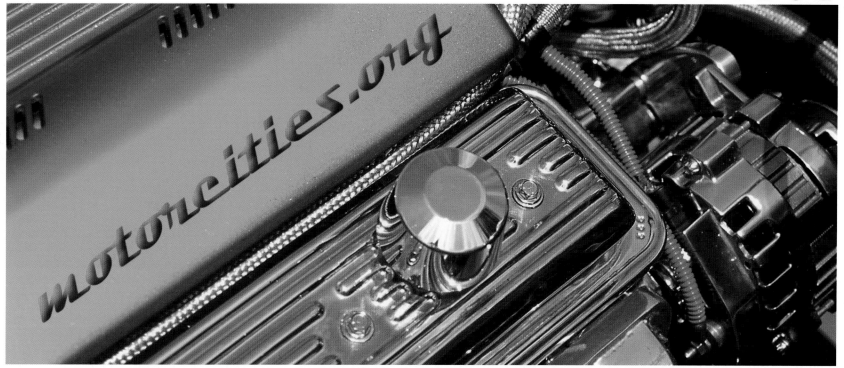

Revving and Reviving Motor City

There is an emerging bright side to the woes of Motor City as individuals and organizations are stepping up to the plate to reverse the bleak images of Detroit that a slumping economy – as well as the notoriety of having the highest unemployment and crime rates in the nation – have given.

One such leader is Bill Chapin, son of Roy Chapin Jr., who served as chairman of American Motors Corporation. Bill observed, "Detroit is getting a bum rap right now because of the current situation. But if you separate the current malaise from the larger picture of Detroit being the center of the automotive universe, things don't look so bad."

In 2005, Chapin convinced representatives and curators from the world's motor museums to come to Detroit to attend the biennial World Forum for Motor Museums convention, which succeeded in propping up Detroit's image on the global stage. His inspiration and ideas are now focused on the Automobile National Heritage area, which uses tourism as a magnet to lure out-of-town and international visitors to the region.

"We celebrate a living industry – one with a proud heritage and a bright future. The automobile industry is as important to our communities today as it was 100 years ago."

Gary Familian, Director
Automobile National Heritage Area

With a similar effort, the 13th annual Woodward Dream Cruise is gearing up to keep the focus on Motor City with a bit of cruise history that started as a way to raise funds for a children's soccer field but has become the world's largest one-day celebration of car culture. It now attracts more than 1.7 million people and 40,000 "dream" cars of all descriptions. Cruisers and spectators follow a 16-mile route that winds through nine Michigan communities and keeps the vision of Motor City alive. Best of all, it's a "free ride" for families and participants due to the generous support of involved and motivated sponsors.

All are important components for "The Year Of The Car" celebrations in 2008. I urge you to attend and participate.

Drive in Peace,

1

Automobile Quarterly

The Connoisseur's Publication of Motoring
– *Today, Yesterday, and Tomorrow* –

GERRY DURNELL
Editor & Publisher

KAYE BOWLES-DURNELL
Associate Publisher

JOHN C. DURNELL
Chief Operations Officer, Technical Editor

TRACY POWELL
Managing Editor

JOHN EVANS
Chief Financial Officer

DAN BULLEIT
Art Director

ROD HOTTLE
Administrative Assistant

ROBIN JEFFERS
Customer Service

L. SCOTT BAILEY
Founding Editor and Publisher

Contributing Photographers
PHIL BERG
GAVIN FARMER
MICHEL ZUMBRUNN

Contributing Writers
PHIL BERG
GRIFFITH BORGESON
LEIGH DORRINGTON
GAVIN FARMER
TRACY POWELL
L. SPENCER RIGGS
PETER RÜTIMANN

www.autoquarterly.com

ISBN 1-59613-056-3
(978-1-59613-056-2)

Printed in Korea

Contents

VOLUME 47, NUMBER 4 • FOURTH QUARTER 2007

Cover: "Dream Car"

Left: "Toyland Delivery"

ALFA ROMEO

SALON

BY FERDINAND HEDIGER
PHOTOGRAPHY BY MICHEL ZUMBRUNN

Hundreds of articles and dozens of books have been written on the famous marque from Milan. It would be pointless to rewrite the development and history of the touring, sporting and racing Alfa Romeos, to dwell on the brilliant technical specifications or the qualifications of the outstanding engineers in charge of design. This article therefore is a more personal approach to celebrated Alfa Romeo models over the years. From the archive of the well-known Swiss photographer of fine cars, Michel Zumbrunn, we present sculptures in metal created by masters of engineering and design.

Above: 1925 Alfa Romeo RL Sport. Opposite: 1932 Zagato 6C1750 SS.

From the very beginning Alfa Romeo has built touring and sports cars for enthusiastic drivers all over the world. Even the most docile versions had extraordinary road and handling qualities paired with sophisticated engineering. The sporting and competition models, usually based on the bread-and-butter types, were fitted with high-performance engines and improved chassis. Only a few marques can claim to have produced hardly any dull cars over a period of close to 100 years. Despite many ups and downs in its history, Alfa Romeo always kept its goal in mind to develop and manufacture cars for a demanding and sport-minded clientele.

The racing debut took place in the sixth Targa Florio in 1911. The 24hp model driven by Nino Franchini with Giuseppe Campari in the mechanic's seat ran out of road when in second position. The new cars from Milan still left an excellent impression. The company and private owners would continue to participate in circuit and hill climb races and many forms of motor competition right into modern times.

TIPO RL BY MEROSI

After producing a variety of cars with engines of 2.5- to 6.3-liter capacity prior to WWI the new Type RL was developed in 1920-21. The engine was a six-cylinder inline with overhead valves operated by pushrods and a capacity of 2916 cc. Deliveries began one year later and the car was available in three distinct versions. The basic RL Normale received touring bodies. Its engine developed 56 hp. The RL Sport and RL Super Sport, mostly with open torpedo and spider coachwork, offered up to 83 hp. Production continued until 1927 and a total of 2,640 cars were manufactured and sold in Italy and abroad.

His Highness Maharaja Aga Khan also fell in love

with the RLSS. In 1925 he ordered a torpedo with four seats by the renowned coachbuilder Ercole Castagna. The aluminum body was brushed and then plug-polished, a technique sometimes used on sports cars of the period. Despite its relatively small-capacity engine the Alfa Romeo RLSS was a lively sports car with a top speed of about 80 mph. Aga Khan, who was a sophisticated car lover with many fine vehicles in his garages, wrote to the works: "One of the best cars I ever have driven." From 1925 on, the Alfa Romeo emblem, here placed on both sides of the V-shaped radiator, was framed by the laurel to commemorate the winning of the first marque World Championship in Grand Prix racing.

The author remembers another RLSS coachbuilt by the small Swiss company Charles Heber of Geneva. For a long time this car was the treasured property of a Swiss enthusiast. It was driven in wintertime with snow-chains fitted. The car was sold to a collector in Germany. The car is still very much in original condition with a wonderful patina.

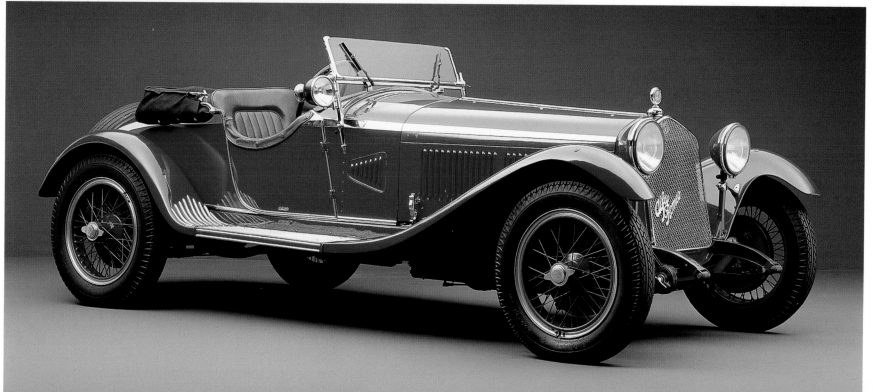

6C1500 AND 6C1750

Late in 1924 the management of Alfa Romeo asked Vittorio Jano to develop a new light passenger car with a medium-size engine. A few months later the prototype of the 6C1500 was shown for the first time at the Milan Show. It was immediately hailed by the experts as a very attractive touring and sports car with many advanced features. Yet, deliveries did not begin until 1927. Meanwhile the original sohc engine of the normal touring version was developed into a dohc unit for the sport model. A Super Sport model could also be fitted with a supercharger. Output increased from 44 hp to 84 hp. The versions with high-performance engines were immediately entered in a great many competitions for sports cars, where they often proved the fastest in the field. In 1929 the range obtained new, enlarged engines. These wonderful cars received the designation 6C1750 Turismo, Gran Turismo, Sport, Gran Sport and Super Sport.

One of the more spectacular events was certainly the Mille Miglia of 1930, won by the Italian daredevil Tazio Nuvolari after a great battle with Achille Varzi on a similar supercharged 6C1750 Gran Sport testa fissa. Varzi had started 10 minutes ahead of Nuvolari. When, after 16 hours of all-out driving, the latter saw the taillights of his adversary less than half a mile ahead, he wanted not only to win but wanted to arrive at the finishing line before Varzi. "It was at this point that the legend was born that Nuvolari closed up on his rival, with headlights off (it was dusk), switched them on suddenly as he overtook Varzi near Lonato on the outskirts of Brescia. Nuvolari went on to finish the race in record time. He and his partner, Guidotti, were the first drivers to have exceeded an average of 100 km/h (60 mph)." This dramatic report was from the pen of Conte Giovanni Lurani.

8C2300 SUPERCHARGED

To maintain the superiority in sports car races a more potent model was developed. The resulting 8C2300, only available with supercharged

Above and opposite: 1933 8C2300 convertible by Pininfarina.

8

dohc engines, became the most successful Alfa Romeo sports car of the early 1930s. The 8C2300 was of course a thoroughbred sports car with all the ingredients of a winner. The powerful engine mated with light bodies made it very fast, demanding drivers with high skill and quick reflexes. The list of success in minor and major competition is nearly endless and includes Mille Miglia, Tourist Trophy, local and national events in many countries. The famous 24-hour race of Le Mans was won four times in a row from 1931-34.

In the 1970s a beautiful roadster of 1934 with Pininfarina body participated in private meetings at the Lake of Lucerne. To many it was a pinnacle of superbly sophisticated engineering with its fabulous engine and chassis, a sporty shape and harmonious lines of a masterful design by the great artist in coachbuilding. For pure sports, the 8C2300 with Spider coachwork by Touring or Zagato filled the bill admirably.

To this day the various versions of the 6C1500/1750 and the 8C2300 are among the most admired cars participating in the historic Mille Miglia but also in the famous Concours d'Elégance from Pebble Beach to Villa d'Este.

THE MAGNIFICENT PREWAR 8C2900

Developed as a successor of the 8C2300 that had won fame in the great sports car events for Alfa Romeo and many private drivers, the factory showed the first 8C2900A at the Paris Salon in October 1935. The sales leaflet contained photographs of the chassis, a sleek roadster, and a two-seater sports racing model. One year later the 8C2900B was launched at the Paris Salon. Simon Moore's book *The Immortal 2.9* provides detailed information on the development and history of the approximately 43 cars which Alfa Romeo manufactured until 1939.

Experts are united in their opinion that the Alfa Romeo 8C2900 was probably the fastest and certainly among the most beautiful sports cars of prewar days. It was a thoroughbred with very advanced technical

Alfa Romeo 8C2900B Spider by Touring, 1938. A masterpiece.

specifications. The eight-cylinder inline dohc engine was fitted with twin superchargers and output reached 225 hp. The chassis had independent suspension front and rear, excellent hydraulic brakes with huge drums in the 19-inch wire-spoke wheels.

As the earlier models, the 8C2900 was highly successful in many national and international events. It brought Alfa Romeo no less than four consecutive victories in the 1935-38 Mille Miglia events, the last one with a record average speed of 84.4 mph, which lasted until 1953.

The author had his first encounter with these superb sports cars at the tender age of 14 when visiting his first automobile race in Berne in 1948 with his father. In the national sports car event, which regularly preceded the Grand Prix, both Swiss drivers – Paul Glauser and Jean Studer – drove 8C2900s with modified bodywork. They crossed the finish line in first and second position with less than three seconds separating them. Willy Peter Daetwyler on a 6C2500SS gave his debut in Berne but could not do better than fifth place. One year later Daetwyler scored his first win in his recently acquired Alfa Romeo Tipo 412 sports racing car with the V12 engine of 4½ liters in an 8C2900 chassis. For the next few years and up until 1954 the combination of this powerful car and brave driver proved to be nearly unbeatable in Swiss sports car racing. There were constant rumors as to the true power of the supercharged engine, which finally must have been well in excess of 250 hp. Having regularly watched the practice sessions and races of Berne, the roaring, red-and-white Alfa Romeo 412 of Daetwyler remains an automotive highlight of the author's youth.

One specific Alfa Romeo 8C2900 that caught the imagination of any enthusiast certainly is the out-of-this-world sports racing berlinetta by Touring for the 1938 Le Mans race. It was driven by the team of Raymond Sommer and Clemente Biondetti, both experienced pilots. On Sunday morning the dominating Alfa Romeo was leading its closest competitors by more than 100 miles. Sommer put up the fastest lap at 98.18 mph. About six hours before the finish, either the gearbox gave up or a valve had broken and the car was

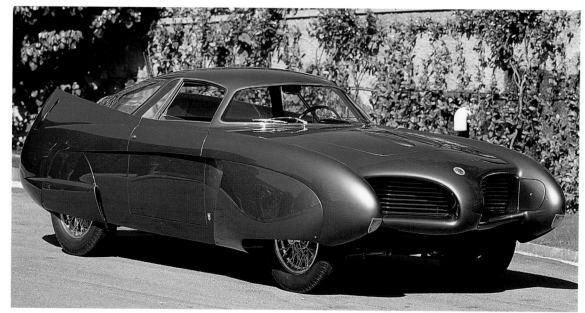

ally described as "disastrous" and "catastrophic." "The 408 cars and a few aero engines which it built in that year did little to keep the foundering company afloat," wrote Griff Borgeson. The government stepped in and saved the company. A more economically produced model was needed. Sales increased slowly and through 1938 a total of 1,606 cars and chassis of the 6C2300 were manufactured. As race participation was considered vital for the marque, several types of racing cars and the 8C2900 were developed and produced at high cost in very small numbers.

From 1939 on, and especially in the postwar years, the 6C2500 in various versions replaced the original models. Power output rose to 87 hp and up to 145 hp in the few works competition cars. Production remained limited. With 2,594 units of the 6C2500, Alfa Romeo was only a minor player in a growing market. The closed cars with coach and berlina bodies were mostly produced by the factory. In 1947 Robert Braunschweig, chief editor of the Swiss weekly

Above: The Alfa Romeo B.A.T.S. Right: 1954 Giulietta 1300 Spider.

out of the race. If the photographs of this car are fascinating, the car itself, now belonging to the Alfa Romeo museum, is even more breathtaking. The author saw it for the first time at Villa d'Este in 2001 when a photograph of it was taken by Michel Zumbrunn, together with Carlo Felice Bianchi Anderloni, the former boss of Carrozzeria Touring, Milan.

A "SOFTER" APPROACH WITH 6C2300/2500

When the company launched the new line 6C2300 in 1934 there was an uproar among the dyed-in-the-wool Alfisti. After the light 6C1750 and 8C2300 with high-performance engines, the new model did not look very promising. It still had an engine with twin-overhead camshafts but now these were operated by a chain and the output was a modest 68 hp compared to the 142 hp of the supercharged eight-cylinder of similar capacity.

Alfa Romeo's overall condition in 1933 was gener-

This '54 Giulietta 1300 Spider by Bertone is the prototype on chasis 002

Automobil Revue, fell in love with the 6C2500 Sport "Freccia d'Oro" with Alfa Romeo coachwork. It was an impressive, beefy coach, the steel body welded to the frame. It was horribly expensive at about $10,000, compared to $3,930 for the Buick Special Series 50. Braunschweig drove this car for many years and kept it even after he had long switched to other cars for everyday use. In the office of *Automobil Revue* the car, due to its bulkiness, was nicknamed the "aircraft carrier" by the staff. It is still in possession of Braunschweig's son and sometimes seen in Swiss meetings.

Many 6C2300/2500 cars were coachbuilt by Italian and foreign companies. Apart from Touring, Milano, Pininfarina did plenty of coachbuilding on these models. Stabilimenti Farina,

Colli, Balbo and Boneschi tried their hands on the chassis as well. They were also chosen by Graber, Tüscher and Worblaufen in Switzerland. Some of these cars are the most beautiful to bear the emblem of Alfa Romeo.

A fine, silver coupé by Superleggera Touring encountered in the city of Zürich in the late 1950s is well remembered. A ravishing young blonde was at the wheel. Taking up the pursuit, the author was unsure whether the car or the lady was more attractive. After nearly half an hour's driving through increasingly better quarters of the town, both came to a halt in front of an expensive home. No, the author did not muster the courage to talk to the woman, but at least he could take a good look and take a few pictures of the car.

1900 AND DERIVATES

In view of the limited sales potential of the 6C2500, once again a new, smaller and less-expensive model was developed. In 1950 the Alfa Romeo 1900 berlina was launched. It was the first mass-produced model with united construction of chassis and body, which offered a substantial weight and cost reduction. The engine was the first four-cylinder inline in many years, but with its twin overhead camshafts and alloy head it was typically Alfa Romeo. The basic version yielded 90 hp, the twin carburettor T.I. and Sprint offered 100 hp. The new model was favorably welcomed by press and clientele. Shortly after the start of deliveries of the berlina in 1951, the very handsome

Alfa Romeo Giulietta 1300 Spider by Pininfarina, 1955. The prototype on chasis 003.

Beautiful, inside and out: the 1955 Alfa Romeo 1900 Zagato.

did not see regular production. Happily some of these experimental cars survived and are shown in exhibitions and concours d'elegance.

A superb competition car was the handsome 1900 SSZ Super Sprint Zagato of 1955, originally the property of the Swedish racing driver Joakim Bonnier. Bonnier started his career driving this car in national and international events before switching to other marques and Formula 1 racing.

The Alfa Romeo 1900 enabled the company to break into quantity production. In 10 years, through 1959, a total of 21,304 cars were delivered.

Sprint coupé by Touring, Milano and a cabriolet by Pininfarina were presented. Soon various coachbuilders proposed special-bodied Alfa Romeo 1900s.

Probably the most exciting were the three different versions of the futuristic B.A.T. by Bertone. The first, B.A.T. 5 designed by Franco Scaglione, was originally shown at the Turin Motor Show of 1953. Featuring an aerodynamic form with wheel spats front and rear and twin tailfins curving inward, a long, flat engine bonnet and two big radiator openings, it was a break away from standard practice. A year later Bertone presented the B.A.T. 7, which was a further step into the future. In 1955 the B.A.T. 9 also designed by Scaglione was

again shown in Turin. It was more moderate and closer to production possibilities with smooth flanks and less-pronounced tailfins.

To explore possible participation in the Sports category at racing events, the works built a few prototypes of the "Disco Volante" (Flying Saucer) based on the 1900 platform. These purely competition-oriented spiders and one coupé with sophisticated aerodynamic bodies on tubular space frames by Touring had their engines tuned to 158 hp. They were supplemented by four 2000 Sportivas with open and coupé bodies by Bertone, as well as by a handful of three-liter six-cylinder models. All of them remained prototypes and

Giulietta and Giulia

With the Giulietta in 1954, Alfa Romeo presented a truly affordable sports car to the public. It took the hearts of sport drivers by storm and remained a favorite for the next 10 years. Interestingly, the Sprint coupé version by Bertone was shown first and the berlina with factory body, as well as the cabriolet by Pininfarina, followed one year later. The tiny 1300cc four-cylinder dohc engine offered 80 hp in the basic model and 90 hp in the Veloce version with twin carburetors. Road performance was lively and close to that of the 1900 series.

Especially designed by Scaglione for the U.S. market, one of the earliest Giulietta platforms (002) received a beautiful Spider body by Bertone. Pininfarina simultaneously manufactured a spider on platform 003. After having spent most of their lives in America, both prototypes returned to Europe a few years ago. These unique, pretty cars are now in an Alfa Romeo collection. Apparently there were two more spider prototypes made by Bertone and Pininfarina that remain in the America. As is well known, the production contract for the Giulietta Spider finally went to Pininfarina.

Another one-off Giulietta in the collection mentioned is the "La Goccia" (The Teardrop). It is the first car designed by the young Giovanni Michelotti and saw the light of this world in 1961. Originally an ordinary Sprint Veloce, it was transformed by Zagato as a SVZ before it was rebodied by Michelotti and prepared by Virgilio Conrero to become the Giulietta SV "La Goccia." With its aerodynamic aluminum body of 1,650 pounds and a tuned engine yielding 126 hp, its top speed was timed at 136 mph on the speed section of the Monza racecourse. It was a pure competition coupé that could hold its own against the strong Zagato-bodied SZ on several occasions.

Both the Giulietta and its successor the Gulia were very successful. A total of 177,690 of the former and 265,877 of the latter were produced between 1954 and 1972. In addition, 18,410 Alfa Romeo 2000 and 2600 of various types were manufactured in the same period. The company had hit its stride and was a serious contender on the market, not just in sporting events.

1961 Alfa Romeo Giulietta coupé designed by Giovanni Michelotti, the first of his prolific career.

Alfa Romeo 8C "Brera" Concept Car by Italdesign, 2002. Designed by Fabrizio Giugiaro, this was the first prototype with the V8 engine of 4254 ccm tranversally mounted.

the Turin Show of 1968 a very futuristic idea car by Bertone, based on this model, the 33/2 "Carabo" was shown. Its wedge shape and the up-and-forward opening doors make it a stunning car even today. Pininfarina also gave it a try and presented its 33/2 one year later at Turin. Wherever these idea cars are shown they immediately draw a crowd of admirers.

EVERYDAY ALFA ROMEOS

The box-like berlinas and their relatives – the attractive coupé by Bertone and spider by Pininfarina of the 1750 and 2000 series – were added to the Giulia from 1967 onward. In 1972 the all-new Alfetta followed. It boasted many advanced features combined with trusted and reliable components used before by the company. The transaxle principle, with the five-speed gearbox fitted at the rear and in unit with the differential, gave an excellent weight distribution. The De Dion rear axle further enhanced

CANGURO, CARABO AND COMPANY

Based on the Giulia 1600 the TZ 1 (Tubolare Zagato) was developed and became available in 1963. One year later Bertone surprised the visitors of the Turin Show with a lightweight super sports coupé, the TZ 2 "Canguro," with a very smooth, streamlined body. For more than 30 years the car was not seen in public. It was on display at the Concours d'Elegance of Villa d'Este in 2005, brought to the event by its owner from Japan.

For competing in the Sports Prototype class in 1967, Alfa Romeo produced the Tipo 33 with a new V8 two-Liter engine with four overhead cams placed mid-ship in the race car, which came in coupé and spider form. It was most successful, winning 15 overall and six class victories in 1968 and continuing to win races in subsequent years. The slightly de-tuned Tipo 33/2 Stradale received two-seater coupé bodies by Scaglione. At

Alfa Romeo 8C Spider by the works, 2006. Presented for the first time in Europe at Villa d'Este and winning the design trophy.

the safe handling and good road behavior. The author owned one of the early 1.8-liter berlinas and enjoyed it thoroughly, until it started to rust badly, which was the only serious drawback of a great family touring car.

In the 1970s Alfa Romeo had a staggering variety of models and body types with Giulia, 2000, GT, Alfetta, new Giulietta, Montreal, Alfa 6 and the all new Alfasud. "The Alfasud is the first Alfa Romeo with front-wheel drive. It was produced as an economical car of superior quality, designed for motorists in the medium-income bracket desirous of driving an authentic Alfa Romeo," wrote Luigi Fusi. A new factory was built near Naples expressly for quantity production of the Alfasud. The new car debuted at the Turin Motor Show of 1971 and deliveries began in 1973.

When the author replaced his Alfetta in 1980, a test run of the Alfasud with the 1.5-liter flat-four engine was as convincing as the six-year warranty against rust. This little berlina was pure joy to drive. It was cheap, light, reliable and quite a bit faster that expected. The Alfasud was strictly on his side in awkward situations on the road.

8C Brera – trophy bagger at Villa d'Este

Over the years several concept and idea cars based on Alfa Romeo models were presented at motor shows by various coachbuilding companies and design studios. Most of them, after being in the limelight for a short while, were soon forgotten.

Italdesign showed the 8C Brera prototype, designed by Fabrizio Giugiaro, with a powerful, transversally mounted V8 engine of 4254 cc, for the first time at the Salon of Geneva in spring 2002. Things were different this time. Rumor had it that Alfa Romeo might consider putting it into regular production. Just a few weeks later it was entered in the newly launched category of concept cars in the Villa d'Este event. It was greatly admired in its home country and obtained the design prize in the contest.

In 2004 another 8C, now with a new coupé body developed in the design department of Alfa Romeo, won the design trophy again. In 2006 at Villa d'Este the factory presented the new 8C spider, designed at the works with the American market in mind. It was awarded the coveted trophy for a third time.

PRESENT RANGE

Since 1986 Alfa Romeo has been part of the Fiat group. The marque offers a wide range of cars for many purposes and budgets. While produced in relatively large quantities – total output in 2006 was approximately 158,000 cars – Alfa Romeo successfully maintains the image of manufacturing sports cars. Owners all over the world confirm the excellent performance and love the distinguished lines of the various body types developed by the works design department, Bertone or Pininfarina.

Present basic models have their engines built in transversally and have front-wheel drive. The exceptions are the 4x4 Q4 types. The economy model 147 is available as a three- or five-door sedan. The models 159 and 166 are four-door sedans, the former also available as an attractive sports wagon. The GT and Brera are coupés and the range is complemented by the traditional spider. The engines' available range is from 1.6- to 2.2-liter four-cylinder types and a 3.2-liter V6 model with gasoline injection and 1.9- to 2.4-liter turbo diesels. Power output is from 105 to 260 hp.

In addition, the new model 8C Competizione with a V8 powerplant of 4.7 liters yielding 450 hp and rear-wheel drive on the Maserati basis was launched at the Geneva Salon in spring 2007. It is a superb coupé designed by the works design team, and a spider is in preparation. It is with this platform that Alfa Romeo plans to return to the American market some time in 2008, 13 years after withdrawing from the United States. The 8C will be built in a limited-production run of 500 units to be distributed in several key markets worldwide. The company has also announced that it will release the 159, Brera and Spider in 2009, after they receive mid-life styling and technical updates.

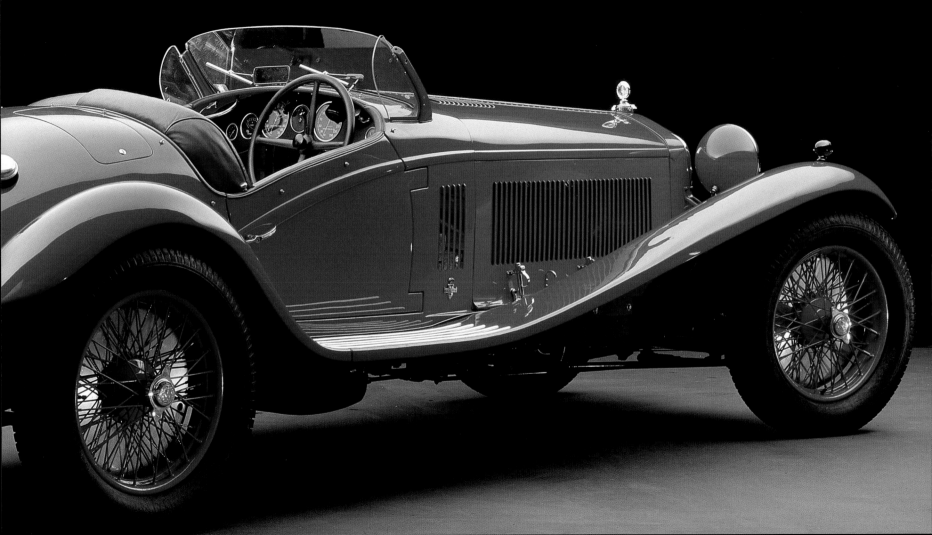

THE SCHOOL OF TRADITION

Imbedded in Alfa Romeo lore, Orazio Satta's legacy defines the postwar automotive tradition of Alfanord, and his contributions to Alfasud were of utmost importance. He stands as the legendary creative giant of Alfa Romeo history as a whole, and to list all for which the firm is indebted to him would be an impossible task. We will attempt, however, to present the highlights of his busy tenure.

BY GRIFFITH BORGESON Adapted from *The Alfa Romeo Tradition*

The emergence of Alfa Romeo as a force in the world passenger car industry began with the volume-produced Tipo 1900 of 1950. More than 19,000 of those cars of all-new design were built, in contrast with an annual average of 396 vehicles built for an elite clientele between 1930 and 1940. Yet the 1900 carried forward uncompromisingly the thoroughbred traditions of the marque.

From that modest start the original Giulietta was developed, and from it the Giulia, the 1750, the Alfetta, and more recently the 75 and the 90. These machines and all of their many variants pertain to a single fundamental concept of what a fine but economically accessible road vehicle should be. They pertain to the Satta school. That school or philosophy rests upon

One of Orazio Satta's most memorable creations was the Disco Volante, the Spyder shown here and the coupe shown on the opening page. These prototypes were based on the 1900 platfrrom with engines tuned to 158 hp.

two traditions, the older of which is the Alfa Romeo mystique itself. Of it, Ing. Orazio Satta told the author, during an interview in 1970:

"Alfa Romeo is not merely a maker of automobiles; it truly is something more than a conventionally built car. There are many automotive makes, among which Alfa Romeo stands apart. It is a kind of affliction, an enthusiasm for a means of transport. It is a way of living, a very special way of perceiving the motor vehicle. What it is resists definition. Its elements are like those irrational character traits of the human spirit which cannot be explained in logical terms. They are sensations, passions, things that have much more to do with man's heart than with his brain.

"Of course some of the elements are purely mechanical and are easy enough to identify. They are concepts which arise from the question of motor racing, where their sort of excellence is necessary. We have always held it to be necessary that they should be transmitted, in the best way, to the cars that we sell – braking, roadholding, steering, the feel of the car in the hands of he who drives it. Those things always have been a tradition with us, a thing that we always have sought to provide in our cars."

The other tradition stems from the company's activ-

ity as a major producer of aircraft engines – a decade of highly specialized experience that ended with the bombing of the Il Portello works in Milan on October 1944. Of those days Satta said:

"Aeronautical technology had, over automotive technology, the great superiority of the necessity of absolute reliability and thus the need for much greater planning and application. It required concepts of a much more developed and sophisticated technical character because, naturally, the reliability and therefore the safety of an aircraft should be as absolute as possible. Beyond that, all of the branches of science and technology which were necessary for keeping abreast in aero engines were, for me and all of us, a very important school. This is why, when we had finished with aero engines at the end of the war, we were able to transfer all those systems to the design of new automobiles. I think that it was done at just the right time."

At that epoch, aside from engine design, only in Germany and the United States had a small amount of real science been applied to the design of the automobile as a whole. When it was decided that Alfa Romeo should resume automotive activity, one of Satta's early initiatives was the setting up of a program for scientific research on vehicle dynamics. In doing this, he had from the outset the collaboration of a highly trained young graduate engineer named Erwin Landsberg. Taking the existing 6C 2500 as a base, they started from various conditions of tire loading under acceleration, braking and cornering and calculated them back to all parts of the car. A growing body of important new knowledge of a scientific nature was accumulated in this way. It went into the design of the Alfa Romeo 1900: a most outstanding all-new vehicle. It was all Satta – and was the parent of all subsequent passenger cars designed and built at Il Portello and at the new factory at nearby Arese.

The 1900 was the embodiment of the basic Satta concept of what a volume-produced Alfa Romeo should be. It should have the performance characteristics upon which much of the marque's reputation rested. It should not be too expensive. Up to this point, the

grand maximum of components for cars of the marque had been manufactured, at great cost, by the company itself. This included such elements as shock absorbers, brakes, clutch, steering and so on. Now the product, while retaining its traditional character, should utilize the greatest possible number of components made by leading specialists: clutches by Borg & Beck, brakes by Girling, bearings by Vandervell, etc. It should be mechanically simple, which favored the choice of the four-cylinder engine. Weight should be kept at the lowest reasonable level, and this for Satta meant aircraft-type monocoque construction. He knew that discipline already and he demanded and obtained optimum torsional rigidity in the new body-frame structure. Here, as elsewhere, he was very much a pioneer.

Satta favored fairly small cars and consistently sought the smallest external dimensions, along with the greatest possible internal space. Aside from the fact that more bulky cars cost and weigh more, Satta saw them as being unsuited to Italian road conditions, and in the beginning Italy was his all-important market. Cars designed to his thinking should be fairly narrow, as well as not too long. Narrowness, while contributing to nimbleness and ease of handling on Italy's abundant narrow roads, also favored efficient penetration of air. Of course Satta had a thorough scientific grounding in aerodynamics and made early use of wind tunnel testing.

Just as the spirited performance made possible by a close power-to-weight ratio was fundamental to the concept, so was outstanding roadholding. This made suspension an object for scientific analysis from the start. Within the frame of reference of cost, simplicity and light weight, the rigid rear axle was found to be unbeatable, and became a hallmark of the school. When even better roadholding could be afforded at higher cost, the Alfetta's De Dion rear axle perpetuated the geometry of the rigid type, while reducing unsprung weight to the ultimate minimum.

Another fundamental factor in Satta's design philosophy was safety and here, too, he was a pioneer. The Giulia, for example, was one of the world's first cars to have a safety body, in the modern sense of designed-in

Giampaolo Garcea was born at Padova on June 10, 1912, and there received his degree in mechanical engineering in 1934. Jobs were quite difficult for young engineers to obtain at the time and, owing to his academic qualifications, he won an Alfa Romeo scholarship at the Politecnico di Torino where, a year later, he received his degree in aeronautical engineering. He and Satta were classmates there, and they became close friends.

As soon as he received his second university degree, Garcea wrote to Alfa's managing director, Ing. Ugo Gobbato, saying that he had

crushability. Satta conceived it as being very rigid in the passenger compartment, but soft at front and rear. The Giulia also had its steering gearbox mounted on the bulkhead, behind the engine, and not in the usual far-forward position. These steps and many like them were taken well before American safety regulations became effective in 1966. When the Giulia crash-test program was begun, very few modifications had to be made to the car in order for it to meet those draconian requirements. Satta innovated never for the sake of innovation, but only for that of genuine improvement. He was not bound to any given configuration of automotive architecture and, at the time of his final illness in the early seventies, had led his team deeply into the development of a transverse-engine, front-wheel-drive, mid-size car that would have the roadholding of an Alfa Romeo.

In spite of the monumental importance of his technical and creative leadership, Orazio Satta shunned personal credit and would not speak of his own contributions. Instead, he gave total credit for the achievements of his administration to the design group that was responsible to him, and to the excellent talents

Top (left to right): Livio Nicolis, Satta and Giuseppe Busso. Above: 1947 6C 2500 Freccia d'Oro. Inset: Giampaolo Garcea.

that supported that group. It consisted of just five men: Garcea, Busso, Colucci, Nicolis and Sanesi, in the order in which he listed them to the author in 1970. Of them he said: "These men and their co-workers are the strength of Alfa Romeo."

Each is very important and merits being known.

completed his studies thanks to the company's generosity; he furthermore offered his services, should they ever be required. To his delight and surprise, he was hired immediately. Thus, in August 1935, at the age of 23, he began work at Il Portello, assigned to the aero engine department.

There he worked under department head Amleto Bossi, perhaps the firm's first great specialist in experimentation with development and testing of engines. Bossi had started with Alfa as a simple workman in 1911, but his remarkable intelligence and productivity of ideas had enabled him to rise to his important level. Garcea expected this veteran to make life difficult for him, a rank newcomer with a head full of book-lore, but he was wrong. Bossi received him with open arms and willingly passed on everything he knew. This was Garcea's first real taste of the remarkable team spirit that prevailed at Il Portello.

The company had been manufacturing a small, seven-cylinder radial engine that Vittorio Jano had designed, but it was obsolescent at birth. To correct this situation, Alfa acquired a license to build the avant-garde Bristol Pegasus which, somewhat modified, resulted in the extraordinarily dependable AR

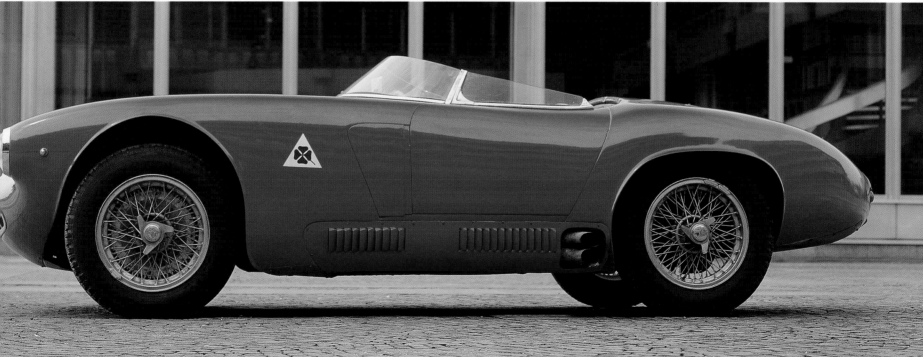

Top: 1950 6C 2500 SS Villa d'Este coupe. Above: 1954 1900 Sport Spider.

Above: 1952 6C 2500 SS. Right: 1951 "Matta" 1900 M military vehicle.

luminaries of the Politecnico di Torino: Panetti and Albenga for aerodynamics, and Capetti for internal combustion engines.

In addition to conducting experiments and tests, the Experimental Service also did research for and proposed solutions to the Design Service. Science-oriented Garcea played an increasingly important role and in 1941 he was placed in charge of the Experimental Service, in which all experimental activities of the company, including those in the aeronautical field, were ultimately combined. Then, in March 1945, the Design and Experimental Department was left without a head when Ricart returned to Spain. Garcea was considered as his replacement, but declined in favor of Satta, who at that point became his chief.

A much greater responsibility of the Experimental Service was research and development for the entire range of the company's postwar production. This extended from 6C 2500 Freccia d'Oro and the 1900 to the Tipo 430, 800 and 900 lines of trucks, then the Romeo van, and diesel, industrial and marine engines and finally to buses and trolley buses. Garcea remained in charge of the Experimental Service until 1956, when he was made the head of a newly formed Study and Research Center. To assist him in his new

126 and 128. Ing. Gobbato also had engaged ex-Isotta Fraschini engineer Giustino Cattaneo who, using the Pegasus as a base, produced the two-row radial AR 135, a marvel of its day. Garcea was co-responsible for the development of these three engines, which became the main stock-in-trade of the firm, in response to growing military demand. Automotive production dwindled to a trickle to 10 cars in 1936.

Cattaneo and Gobbato did not get along, the former leaving Alfa in 1935. Gobbato probably had reason on his side in that case, as he had when Vittorio Jano left two years later. To fill the gap created by this critical exodus, Gobbato engaged Spanish automotive and aeronautical engineer Wifredo Ricart, who was known particularly for his organizational ability.

One of its early expressions was his establishment of a new Design and Experimental Department, which he headed. Under this department were separate Design and Experimental services, each with its own various aeronautical, truck, gasoline engine, diesel and automotive sections. Garcea continued in his good position in the Experimental Service. Ricart also established a Special Studies Service, attached to his Design Service. To head it he hired a brilliant 27-year-old teaching assistant away from the Politecnico di Torino: Orazio Satta. Thus Garcea and his old friend were reunited, and the nucleus was formed for the creative team to come at Alfa. It would include Romolo Gatti and, eventually, Filippo Surace and Livio Nicolis. All of these men had been students of three then-famous

duties, Garcea brought from the Experimental Service Filippo Surace, who had been one of his most valuable collaborators there. Many years later Surace would replace Garcea as head of the Center, and then Satta as director of Design and Development.

Nino Farina in a 159 at the Grand Prix of Italy, August 29, 1951.

Left: 1961 Alfa Romeo Giulietta SZ coupe. Above and top opposite: 1957 1900 CSS coupe. Bottom opposite: 1960 2000 Sprint coupe.

After his move to the Center, Garcea became assistant director of the Design and Experimental Department, at Satta's side. For 20 years he was director of the Fuels and Lubricants Commission of the CUNA, a national association for industrial standardization. He reached retirement age in 1977, but continued to serve the company in a consulting capacity until 1982.

In recent years more than 50 patents have been granted to Garcea by the American and other governments. All have been assigned by him to Alfa Romeo.

GIUSEPPE BUSSO

Giuseppe Busso is really the creator of all the mechanical parts – the chassis and engine – from the 1900 up to the late Alfetta. Along with Garcea, he was one of Satta's two deputies. Satta laid down the general rules and Busso did the designing. He is the father of the mechanical design

of this period." So testified Busso's long-time assistant, Ing. Erwin Landsberg, former assistant director of Alfa Romeo's Vehicular Technical Services.

Busso himself corrects this statement in stressing the great importance of the role played by his chief draftsman, Edo Masoni. It was this man, assisting Busso from 1948 onward,

Above: Consalvo Sanesi in a Tipo 158. Below opposite: Colucci in 1985.

who personally did most of the actual layout work on the drawing board during the early years of postwar production. As the drawing office grew in size, Masoni became its chief.

Busso was born in Turin in 1918. His formal technical training was obtained at the Istituto Industriale di Torino, an institution not empowered to issue degrees in engineering. His endowment for mechanics and mathematics was outstanding. He also was an omnivorous reader, and a command of several languages gave him access to a vast range of technical literature. After doing his military service, Busso went to work in 1937 as an engineering calculator in Fiat's Ufficio Tecnico Motori Aviazione. A consuming passion for the automobile impelled him towards Alfa Romeo, where he

began working at the beginning of 1939. From the start, he was assigned to work at Satta's side, in the Special Studies Service. There he continued to specialize in engineering calculation, in addition to beginning work on the design of aero-engine components, particularly of superchargers.

This still was not the automotive field in which he wanted to be, and in June 1946 Busso resigned from Alfa Romeo in order to head the technical bureau at Ferrari. He left with the explicit understanding that Satta would call him as soon as Alfa should resume automotive activity. That call came in January 1948 and from then until 1977 Busso was responsible for the design of all the mechanical organs of all cars produced at Il Portello and Arese, through to the fuel-

injected V6 and including the racing machines. He enjoyed Satta's total confidence, and a bond of friendship of the strongest sort existed between the two men from the early days of their association. He enjoyed great freedom of decision and choice.

Many cars largely designed by Busso never went beyond the prototype stage. One of the most interesting of these is the Tipo 103 of 1959, a front-wheel-drive car whose transverse 896cc engine developed 52 horsepower and whose body anticipated that of the Giulia. One of the two prototypes built may be seen in the Alfa Romeo Museum today.

Of the Mechanical Parts Design Service, Busso became head in 1952, manager in 1954, assistant director in 1966, director in 1969, assistant central

Left: 1954 2000 Sportiva prototype. Right: 1962 Guilia SS. Below: The 2000 motor, used from 1957 to 1962.

director in 1972, and co-central director in 1973. The working environment was not the same following Satta's death in 1974 and in 1977, a year before he was to reach retirement age, Busso severed all ties with the company. By 1990, still living in Arese, his relationship with Alfa had been positively renewed.

IVO COLUCCI

Ivo Colucci was the other of Satta's top two men in Design. His specialty was body engineering – both structural and styling. Satta himself happened to be strong in both of these fields and was consulted much more by Colucci than by Busso, to whom Satta gave much more free play. But Colucci was a top treater of sheet metal and, as such, an essential and precious member of this small but very creative team.

Colucci was born at Livorno on Sept. 30, 1914, and went to work at Il Portello in 1932 as a worker in the body-building section of the factory. In 1935 he entered the special shop reserved for the construction of experimental coachwork, where he served as a draftsman. In 1937 he was transferred to the main body design office, where he continued to work as a draftsman until 1940, a year during which wartime conditions caused him to be moved to the Cantieri Riuniti dell'Adriatico at Monfalcone. There Colucci began to acquire the knowledge of aircraft fuselage design that would prove to be so valuable when the time came to develop the monocoque structure for the Alfa Romeo 1900.

From Monfalcone, Colucci went on to the huge aircraft factory that Alfa Romeo had recently constructed at Pomigliano d'Arco, near Naples. There he worked as an aircraft draftsman under Ing. Raimondo Gatti, another alumnus of the Turin Polytechnic and friend of Satta. When that plant was destroyed many of the employees, including Gatti and Colucci, were transferred to another company facility, this one at Armeno, in the hills above the Lago d'Orta, just west of Lago Maggiore.

A great part of the design and experimental departments had been decentralized to this location. At

Armeno, Gatti and Colucci were officially assigned to military and aeronautical projects; in reality, they worked on products that the company might produce should events prevent the production of vehicles and engines. They developed such potential merchandise as sheet-metal shutters and cabinets, and electrical domestic appliances.

When the automotive body-design office was re-established in 1946, Gatti and his right-hand man Colucci were integrated into it. It was under Gatti's

Above: 1961 Giulietta Spyder. Bottom right: 1960 Giulietta station wagon.

Above: Vittorio Jano (right) taking delivery of a new Guilietta in 1958, as Satta (center) looks on. Below: The Beatles traveling Italy in an Alfa Romeo. Right: Nicolis in 1985.

direction that the two versions of series-built coachwork for the 6C 2500 Freccia d'Oro were realized, and the first small models for a future monocoque car were submitted to static testing by Garcea. Then Gatti left the company and, at the beginning of 1948, the capable Colucci took over as chief of body engineering. His first prototype for the future 1900 berlina was completed in spring 1950, to be followed by its line of ever more refined descendants.

Ivo Colucci no doubt was admired by Satta for his extreme modesty, as well as for his professional ability and solid contributions to Alfa Romeo. He became manager of his department in 1954 and bore the title of director when he left the company in 1977.

LIVIO NICOLIS

Livio Nicolis was born in Brescia on Dec. 2, 1916. His family then moved to Verona and he did his first two years of engineering studies at nearby Padova. Because of his strong interest in aviation he went to Turin (in those days a degree in aeronautical engineering could be had only at the Polytechnic there and in Rome) and in 1940 he received a degree in mechanical and industrial engineering, sub-category aeronautical. He needed another year for his full aeronautical degree and registered for it, but the wartime situation suggested that he would do better to get into industry without delay. He applied at Alfa Romeo, was hired and assigned to the aero-engine experimental department – one of the places in the world where he would like most to be. His boss, Giampaolo Garcea, was just 4½ years his elder, and the two men became fast friends from the first.

Still being eminently eligible for military service, Nicolis participated in a competitive examination in which his high score won him the rank of lieutenant in the Italian Air Force, assigned to … Alfa Romeo. This happy arrangement did not last long, whereupon he was sent, in an inspector's capacity, to the Savoia Marchetti company, an aircraft manufacturer at Sesto Calende, about 50 km west of Milan. He remained there until the fall of Italy, when the German army occupied the zone. Members of the Italian military who had left jobs in industry were permitted to return to them if they wished, and in 1944 Nicolis was back working for Garcea. He had married and made his home in Sesto, and for seven years he commuted between there and Il Portello by rail. During that period he probably did the equivalent of five times around the world by train.

Nicolis lived the early formative period of the new Alfa Romeo Automotive Experimental Center. At the outset, he was one of many ordinary employees, gaining experience in every sort of experimental work that went on at the plant. Finally, in 1947, he was promoted to the rank of assistant to the chief, and Garcea put him in charge of the company's racing cars, the team of Formula 1 "Alfetta" 158s. He became responsible for all racing activity, including the experimental development of the various cars, tests at Monza and many other venues, the organization of all this activity, and transport of the cars. Under what he called "the superguidance of Ing. Satta," he became the effective technical director of racing operations generally. From 1947 through 1951 he traveled throughout Europe with some of the finest racing drivers and what manifestly were the finest racing cars in the world at that time. He had the rare satisfaction of playing a key role in the increase of his machines' output from 240 hp at 7500 rpm to 430 at 9500 and the consequent winning of two World Championships. He said, with consummate understatement: "All that was a very sympathetic period, which I still recall with pleasure."

Satta took the most intense interest in the performance of the 158/159s, both from the technical standpoint and from that of building the image of the marque and of generations of Alfa Romeo production cars that were yet to be born. He worked closely with Nicolis on the entire Formula 1 program. They drove to most of the Grands Prix together, often sharing the same hotel room. A fraternal rapport flowered between Satta, Garcea and himself that Nicolis described as having been a perfect "symbiosis." The faith of each in the other grew to be total.

The era of the Formula 1 adventure was followed by the creation of a Special Experimental Service, of which Nicolis was the head. Its function was to look after the needs of competition-minded clients who sought assistance, as well as those of the factory's own experimental and small-series high-performance cars, such as the "Disco Volante" variants. This new department was entirely separate from Garcea's Experimental Service, which was devoted to the development of production cars.

In 1956, Garcea was appointed head of the Study and Research Center, an entity concerned with long-range planning and such problems as air-pollution control. At this time the two separate experimental services were fused, with Nicolis in charge of the new organism. Never losing his interest in the competition sector, he continued in his new capacity until his retirement in 1980. Up through the late 1980s, he, Garcea and others of the old guard continued reuniting on the anniversary of Satta's death to hold a memorial mass for their departed chief and friend.

A unique test of the wintertime acceleration of the Guilia 1600 ti.

A church official driven in a 2600 during a public appearance.

CONSALVO SANESI

Consalvo Sanesi did not possess the cultural refinement nor the intellectual baggage of the other members of the team, but his great native intelligence, skill and appalling courage put him on an equal level with all the rest.

Sanesi was born at Terranova Bracciolini, a few miles south of Florence, on March 28, 1912. His parents eventually moved to the nearby city, where they became acquainted with the family of noted racing driver Gastone Brilli Peri. By 1928 Sanesi, then 17, had a grave case of the racing virus and his dream was to work for Alfa Romeo. His parents asked Brilli Peri if there was anything that he might be able to do.

It happened that this man, the winner of the 1925 Grand Prix of Italy and almost-winner of the first Mille Miglia in 1927 – with Alfa Romeos, of course – had need of a mechanic to ride with him and to look after his cars. He arranged with Vittorio Jano for the young man to be given a try at Il Portello. He learned to work on racing cars unofficially that winter, finally going on the company payroll in February 1929. He worked for and rode with his patron until Brilli Peri's death at the wheel of a Talbot-Darracq in the trials for the Grand Prix of Tripoli on March 28, 1930. Sanesi returned to Jano, asking what he should do now. "Do you like your work?" the great man asked. Being told that he adored it, Jano said: "Fine. You will be the mechanic of some other driver."

Sanesi was assigned successively to Campari, Borzacchini and Zehender. He became an expert mechanic and he gained an encyclopedic knowledge of how to handle high-performance machinery at speed. This life continued until Alfa Romeo came entirely under state ownership in 1933, when racing activity was transferred to the Scuderia Ferrari in Modena. Jano gave Sanesi his choice of following the cars there or of remaining at Il Portello as a test driver of production cars, working under the great veteran Attilio Marinoni. He chose the latter, and in a year or so Marinoni was sent to Modena, his place in Milan being taken by Gianbattista Guidotti. No love was lost between the new capo and the kid, who was condemned to touring the provinces for the next couple of years as a roving troubleshooter calling on concessionaires.

In 1938 racing operations were moved back to Il Portello, under the aegis of Alfa Corse and the continuing management of Enzo Ferrari. At this point Sanesi was contacted by Ing. Gobbato, who said that he wanted to try to develop a few racing drivers out of the firm's testers, and would Sanesi care to be one of that number? The young Tuscan, now 26, jumped at the offer, saying that it had been his long-standing dream. He joined Alfa Corse as test driver/apprentice pilot, along with Emilio Villoresi and a motorcycle racing champion named Giordano Aldrighetti. Sanesi's first racing win came in the "Mille Miglia Africana," the Tobruk Tripoli road race of 1939, in which he drove a 6C 2500SS Corsa with, as his own co-pilot, Mussolini's personal chauffeur, Ercole Boratto. Their average speed was 141.416 km/h (87.875 mph).

Villoresi lost his life at Monza and Aldrighetti at Pescara, both driving Tipo 158 monoposto machines. This left Sanesi rather alone to work out the development of the team cars. On his repatriation from

Stages in the development of the Giulietta Sprint (clockwise from left): Bertone's original prototype, entirely hand-formed; the wooden mock-up that was used as the pattern for the first production cars; the prototype in a completed state.

Left: De Adamavich in a 33 2L at the 1967 Targa Florio. Above: Satta speaking on the 100th annivesary of Giuseppe Merosi in 1973. Opposite: An Alfa Romeo GTA in front of competition at Monza, 1970.

Modena, Marinoni had resumed his role of chief tester over both production and racing cars. In June 1940 he was killed while testing on the autostrada and Sanesi found himself selected to fill the important vacant post. He worked with Ing. Ricart on the development of the early 6C 2500 in its various versions, and also on that of Ricart's very promising but very abortive rear-engine flat-12 Tipo 512 Grand Prix monoposto.

In 1944 Sanesi tested and condemned as being beyond hope the "gazella," Ricart's proposal for a two-liter production car and his swan song at Alfa Romeo.

The war ended. Early in 1946 company president Ing. Pasquale Gallo, as part of the plan to resume the output of production cars, decided upon a return to Grand Prix racing. Early in the war, the 158s and 512s had been hidden with great care and total suc-

cess. Now it was Sanesi's assignment to exhume these machines and, with him driving the truck accompanied by Alfa engineer Pavesi, then head of the Experimental Service, all of the prewar monoposti were recuperated and brought back to Il Portello. Thus began the saga of the postwar success of the Tipo 158/159.

The first postwar Italian race was the circuito di Milano, held in September 1946. The top three fin-

Above left: 1968 GT 1300 Junior coupe. Above right: 1965 TZ 2 coupe (its engine, opposite). Bottom: 1966 1600 Spyder.

ishers were Trossi, Varzi and Sanesi, in that order. International Formula 1 racing got underway in 1947, when Sanesi was 5th in the Swiss GP, 2nd in the Bari GP and 3rd in the Italian GP, in which he turned in the fastest lap. He finished 2nd in the Italian Championship for motor racing. In 1948 he was 4th in the European GP at Berne, 2nd in the French GP at Rheims and 3rd in the Monza GP, in which he again clocked the fastest lap. Then he was absent from the Formula 1 scene until 1951, when he finished 4th in the Swiss GP, 19th in the European at Rheims and 6th in the British at Silverstone. As has been always the case with almost all works teams, finishing positions were fixed, as definitely as possible, before each race. Although his lap times at Monza were within about one second of Fangio's, company employee Sanesi was

under orders not to get in front of the superstars.

His performance was of the same highly respectable order in sports car racing. He finished 2nd in the 1949 Mille Miglia and 1st in the 1950 Coppa Intereuropa at Monza in 1950, when he again did the fastest lap. In 1952 he finished 7th in the Mille Miglia but the following year set a new record for the Brescia-Pescara leg with an average of 175.773 km/h (109.225 mph). He probably would have won the race had his car not lost a front wheel, resulting in one of the five major accidents that he somehow managed to survive.

These sporadic exploits, of course, were only a small part of Sanesi's activity. His full-time occupation was the development, through testing to the absolute limits, of all prototypes for Alfa Romeo racing and production cars. His criteria were those of Alfa tradition at its thoroughbred best, of which he was the high priest and keeper of the flame. Not overly articulate, he was a marvelously sensitive and precise instrument. At a staff meeting, Satta once said to him: "Sanesi, in all the many years that we have been working together you never have given me a wrong judgment."

At the height of his activity, Sanesi had about two dozen men working under him – a few top testers and many "mile eaters." But he always conducted the most difficult and final tests himself, and no car went into production until he had given his "OK. Va Bene. Everything is right. It can be made." This applies also to the Alfasud, the testing and development of which also were conducted by Satta's Experimental Service.

Sanesi was leading in the 12-hour race at Sebring in the United States in 1964 when, leaving the pits near the end of the contest, he was involved in his last and most awful accident. He somehow survived the crash and made an amazing recovery, but he took retirement in 1967 at the age of 56.

ORAZIO SATTA

Orazio Satta Puliga was born in Turin on Oct. 6, 1910. He took his degree in mechanical engineering at the Polytechnic there in 1933 and two years later had his degree in aeronautical engineering. With time out for military service as an artillery officer, he remained at the famous school as a teaching assistant in its aeronautics laboratory until 1939, when he joined Alfa Romeo. In 1946 he was appointed director of design and experimentation. In 1951 he became central director; in 1969 assistant general director. He also served as vice president of the Technical Commission of the CUNA.

Satta was a slender man of medium height, with dark eyes and olive complexion. He had very fine, powerful hands, as sculptors are supposed to have. The black hair of his youth turned silver in his 50s. He had an even, tranquil character and was known never to have raised his voice in anger. He spoke rapidly and eloquently. He had a good command of the English, French and German languages and was well read in their technical literature. He was a person of culture who was widely admired for his human qualities and for his skill as a mediator. He was noted for being fair, just and without pretension. Satta took a lively interest in all those who worked under him, all of whom he knew by their first names. He seemed to seek and inspire confidence and friendship in all of his human relations.

Sanesi, who exchanged these sentiments with Satta, feels that he was "too soft, too nice." This may reflect a certain failure in understanding the subtlety of the man. Ing. Landsberg agrees that he gave the impression of being flexible, but affirms that he was very tenacious and tough. He seems to have exerted considerable influence over top management. His ideas often were contested, but he seemed always to have such good evidence for their validity that they ended up being accepted. He might seem to yield in a dispute, only to come back to the same point later, with a different approach, and win it.

Landsberg feels that a very important element in Satta's career was his gift for what today is called systemic thinking: in an industry populated by specialists in this or that part of the whole, he consistently perceived each given motor vehicle as a global system. This seems to be reflected in the integrity of his products.

One of Satta's very remarkable achievements was the creation of a race of modern, mass-produced motor cars which, depending upon the model, retain or improve upon the competition-bred thoroughbred qualities of Alfa Romeos of the artisan past. Mentality

and philosophy have everything to do with this phenomenon. Another contributing factor, Satta liked to emphasize, was the exacting discipline of aeronautical practice, which permeated his organization from top to bottom. Yet another element was the fact that, as Sanesi testifies, Satta was the most accomplished driver of the company's entire engineering staff. Nicolis refused to ride with Sanesi, but Satta was his serene, frequent passenger. It was routine for Sanesi to demonstrate a quirk of behavior at the limit, then say: "Now you do it, Ingegnere. You will see what I mean." And

Above and below: 1972 Montreal. Right: 1968 Carabo.

Satta would do it very well, making the master tester's insights his own.

Orazio Satta died in Milano in March 1974, after a long and most difficult illness. He is remembered with the greatest esteem as the last of the great individual design chiefs of Alfa Romeo. With his passing the firm's engineering department rapidly took on a highly modern "team" structure. One member of this team, which has evolved into an enormous department, had a familiar ring to this name – he was Giuseppe Satta, Orazio's son. AQ

SATTA'S LEGACY

Following is a partial list of automotive highlights of Orazio Satta's career at Alfa Romeo, beginning when Satta took over as head of the design department:

1946-1951: Conversion of the Tipo 158 to two-stage super charging, followed by conversion to the T.159.

1946: Development of 6C 2500 Freccia d'Oro from prewar base.

1946: 6C 2500 Competition.

1948: 6C 3000 Sports Prototype.

1950: 1900 Berlina and Coupe. Beginning of volume production.

1951: 1900 M (AR 51). Four-wheel drive.

1952: 1900 C 52 Disco Volante 2000.

1952: 3000 CM Disco Volante 3500. Six cylinders.

1952: GP T.160. GP prototype; engine only. Flat-12.

1954: 1900 Super.

1954: 2000 Sportiva; prototype.

1954: Giulietta Sprint.

1954: Romeo van; in gasoline and diesel versions.

1954: 3000 PR. Competition Spider; prototype. Six cylinder.

1955: Giulietta Berlina.

1955: 750 Competizione. Competition Spider; prototype.

1957: 2000. Berlina, Spider, Sprint.

1958: Mille. Diesel truck and bus chassis. Six cylinders.

1960: 103. Transverse engine front-wheel-drive prototype.

1962: 2600. Berlina, Spider, Sprint. Six cylinders.

1962: Giulia 1570.

1963: Giulia TZ.

1964: Giulia 1300.

1964: 1600 Veloce. Spider and Coupe.

1965: Giulia Super.

1965: Giulia GTC. Four-passenger Convertible.

1965: Giulia GTA. Light-alloy Coupe. Dual ignition.

1965: 2600 SZ. Zagato 2 + 2. Six cylinders.

1966: Giulia Sprint GT Veloce.

1966: Duetto 1600 Spider.

1966: 4R Zagato. Semi-replica of Jano 6C 1750.

1966: Giulia Scarabeo prototype.

1966: GT 1300 Junior.

1967: GTA-SA. Supercharged for Group 5 competition.

1967: 33/2-liter Sports prototype. Rear-central V8, dual ignition.

1967: Coupe 33 Stradale. Closed version of same.

1968: 1750 Berlina.

1968: 1750 GT Veloce.

1968: 1750 Spider Veloce.

1968: 1300 Junior Spider.

1968: GTA 1300 Junior. Lightweight Coupe.

1969: Giulia 1600 S.

1969: 33/3-liter Sports prototype. Rear-central V8. Single ignition.

1969: GT 1300 Junior Zagato.

1970: 1750 GT Am and 2000 GT Am. Competition Coupe. Dual ignition.

1970: Montreal. Coupe. V8.

1970: 33/3-liter Sports prototype. Light-alloy tubular chassis.

1970: Giulia 1300 Super.

1970: 2000 Berlina.

1970: 2000 GT Veloce. Coupe 2 + 2.

1970: 2000 Spider Veloce.

1972: Alfetta. De Dion transaxle and clutch at rear.

1972: 1600 Junior Z. Developed from 1300 Junior Zagato.

1972: 33/3-liter Sports prototype. Steel tube chassis.

TOY TREASURE

Art Gallery with
Larry Stephenson

What better way for nostalgia and youthfulness to interact than to paint it the way Larry Stephenson does, with toys of yesteryear as the subject matter. Using methods and media that further differentiate his work, this artist defines a niche.

BY TRACY POWELL

Think back. What was your favorite toy? A dump truck? A pedal car? For you ladies, a doll? Larry Stephenson's was, as a group, robots.

"They were pretty cool back in the fifties," Stephenson said.

From this point of reference we can better understand Stephenson's artistic bent. Growing up in a suburb of Oklahoma City, his earliest artistic influence was his grandmother, who was an artist. He took art lessons and majored in art in college, where he also became an art instructor. In 1993 he left his teaching job at Northern Oklahoma College to work as a freelance illustrator.

But about eight years ago his wife walked into the studio and said, "You know, you really don't have to do this. Maybe you would enjoy just painting for yourself more than painting for art directors."

"When you work with marketing people and art directors, you have to be accustomed to working on their whims and their ideas." Stephenson said. "I didn't find that terrible, and I was paid well for it, but I wasn't painting necessarily what I wanted to paint."

What he wanted to paint was all around him.

"First of all, I like automobiles, and I'm a collector by nature," Stephenson said. "I've been collecting antiques for quite some time. I became fascinated with old tin toys, so I acquired this collection of a variety of tin toys over the years. I had all these toy cars that I had collected over the years and that's where the inspiration came from. I believe very strongly in painting what you know. And the toy cars were something I could relate to firsthand and of course I had models in my studio."

PLAYIN' AROUND

Why toys and not other subject matter, like the more-popular landscape genre?

"I purposely don't want to paint landscapes because there are a lot of landscape artists," Stephenson said. "That's a realm that's pretty much covered. When I started doing what I'm doing right

Opposite: "JuijyFruits." Above: "Blue Boattail Racer."

now with this collection of paintings it was because it was my own idea. I'm sure there are other toy painters out there, but as far as my approach to what I do and the whimsical nature of it, they're my own ideas. They fall into a certain niche that's unique to itself."

Like so many others, his first introduction to toys was what he inherited from his parents. Some of those old toys – especially cars and trucks like Buddy L and Steelcraft – were made out of pressed steel and they were built to last several lifetimes. This age-old quality, which can certainly be appreciated when such items are held, is one of the attributes Stephenson attempts to capture in his paintings.

Memories or other personal ties play a large role in what clients request in their commissioned pieces, prices for which begin at $2,000. One example of how a piece is commissioned is seen with a current customer who owns a Chrysler woodie.

"He and his wife have collected toys that are Chrysler-oriented over the years, as well as gasoline memorabilia, things that have to do with transportation," Stephenson said. "They came to me and asked me to put together a painting that would be my style and wit, and would incorporate a Chrysler woodie toy and a gas station. The gas station had to be a Phillips station because the fellow's father had owned a Phillips

station when he was growing up. That's how it starts."

Stephenson also cleverly works in the clients' names whenever possible.

"I have both the man and woman's first names, so somehow I may play on that and put their names in the painting somewhere. If you notice, sometimes I do comics, and they can be used to incorporate most of these folks' names in there. I have fun with those projects. They're well thought out, and it gives customers something that relates to the automobile that they have."

TOY TIME

Because of the bright colors in his paintings and their whimsical nature, Stephenson's paintings go well in a family room or a game room-type setting. Some people look for them as paintings for a kid's room, "although that's not the primary purpose or reason why I paint them."

"The scene behind or around the racecars – for example the one with the marbles, where the car is racing through all the marbles – puts the toy's size in perspective," Stephenson adds. "The marbles themselves, with the toys, give us scale. The marbles and the comic books are also indicative of that era. There are still lots of comics in the paper today, but they're not as big a deal as they were back then.

"In the fifties, when a lot of those tin toys were made, marbles were another thing that almost every

Left: "Fat Tire." Above: Poster for the Glenmoor Gathering, "Oh Buck." Right: "Tin Men" was an award winner in the 2007 *Watercolor USA* exhibition and selected for use on the cover of the exhibition catalog.

boy carried around in his pocket to school. It takes me back to my childhood."

These elements are also used because of the primary colors that are used in both the lithography on the tin vehicles and the comics. Both were presented in bright primary colors, "so the color seems to work well together in my paintings."

Watercolor works best for Stephenson's presentation. He is currently using a combination of watercolor, gouache and egg tempera, all water-based media. He will often combine whatever is needed to get the effect he wants.

"Watercolor is very challenging," said the artist, who is a member of the American Watercolor Society. "For those who don't paint as a hobby or professionally and have never tried watercolor, it's a little bit less forgiving than oil paints because you can't make the

corrections like you can with other mediums. And I always enjoyed the challenge of watercolor.

"My main objective is to connect with the viewer and to bring enjoyment. I don't think that art necessarily has to have any kind of philosophical or political meaning. I think that art can simply be enjoyed, and I hope that the viewers can connect with my subject matter and maybe just remember their own youth, their own experience."

"What I'm doing really marries a couple of passions for me. I love painting and I wouldn't want to be doing anything else. And I also love collecting. So I'm able to combine both of those passions. Of course, I also enjoy classic automobiles, and in the past I've fixed

up a couple of Chevy pickup trucks, one a 1950 and the other a 1954."

It's all about toys, however, and it has been since the moment his wife nudged him onto a different path. At that moment, Stephenson noticed a 1939 Hawthorne Zep bicycle hanging from the wall of his studio, a bike with a card in the spokes. He recounts that he had not heard the "flicker of the card since I was a kid." But he knew he could easily translate the sound to his painting surface with a flick of the brush.

"Toy collectors understand about passion. It may be the hunt for the rare or the unobtainable. Passion may come in the form of finding the perfect rarity in mint like-new condition. For many it is as simple as never completely letting go of childhood memories." AQ

Left: "For All The Marbles." Above: One of Stephenson's favorite ways to relax is fishing (more precisely, flyfishing). As is often the case, he didn't need to go far to locate the objects that appeared in "Gone Fishin'."

Above: Sportily clad riders on tin motorcycles are captured in vibrant color in "Moto." Collectibles like the Tippco motorcycle in the foreground with bright lithography are ideal for Stephenson's work. Right: "Ground's Eye View."

Larry Stephenson—AWS

PRATT

A COMPLETELY NEW SOLUTION

Educating 21st-century designers in a 19th-century industrial training school may seem to be a contradiction. But as it has been doing for more than 100 years, Pratt Institute continues to successfully teach each student to find a completely new solution to ever-changing creative challenges, including the future of the automobile.

BY LEIGH DORRINGTON

Tucked in the middle of Brooklyn, Pratt Institute is as much a product of New York as the Museum of Modern Art. Above left: Pratt Library around the turn of the century. Above right: The institute's founder, Charles Pratt. Below: The man who brought Pratt into the modern age, Alexander Kostellow.

Pratt Institute provides a peaceful oasis in the center of Brooklyn, N.Y. The quiet, leafy campus is surrounded by the sights and sounds of New York City, as if by siege – noise, construction and traffic, vest-pocket parks and basketball courts with weathered metal backboards tucked into the shadows of the Brooklyn-Queens Expressway.

This is New York, as only New Yorkers know it. A few blocks in one direction Hasidic Jewish fathers walk their children to school hand in hand, distinctive in their long black coats, black hats, beards and un-cut sideburns. Signs offering loft spaces for rent are painted onto the sides of old factory buildings. One block in the other direction brings a visitor onto tree-lined Washington Avenue and Clinton Hill with its stately brownstone townhouses built in the 1800s by millionaires who found a haven from the hectic business of Manhattan.

Charles Pratt made his home here, building mansions on Clinton Avenue for himself and three of his four sons. Pratt also built his business in Brooklyn, the Astral Oil Works, which became part of Standard Oil in 1874. Pratt's philanthropy endowed many Brooklyn institutions, and in 1886 he founded Pratt Institute to train industrial workers for the specialized needs of a changing economy.

More than 25,000 Pratt alumni currently work in design, visual arts, architecture, writing, film, television, theatre and other creative fields. Their accomplishments and accomplishments of those who came before them would fill volumes. Some of the best-known Pratt graduates include artists Ellsworth Kelly and Robert Mapplethorpe. Architects Ralph Applebaum who designed the Clinton Library, Robert

York's historic Rhinelander mansion. Photographers Sylvia Plachy and George Kalinsky. Cartoonists Joseph Barbara of Hannah-Barbara and Edward Koren of *The New Yorker*. Sculptor Beverly Pepper. Tony Award-winning playwright and actor Harvey Fierstein and Oscar-winner Robert Redford, who studied painting at Pratt.

Pratt has taught influential designers in the automobile industry as well. Richard Arbib worked at General Motors and Henney, but spent most of his career as an industry consultant working with independents including Packard, Hudson and American Motors. Read Viemeister, director of styling for Lippincott and Margulies, led the team that created the initial design of the futuristic Tucker automobile working with Budd Steinhilber and Tucker P. Madawick – also both Pratt graduates – and Alex Tremulis at Tucker. William

mid-1990s with sporty, affordable small cars. Recent graduates work throughout the industry.

NEW YORK CITY AND THE AUTOMOBILE

In an era when Mayor Michael Bloomberg proposed a special tax to operate an automobile in parts of New York City – as already imposed in London and other cities – it is perhaps difficult to think of New York as an automotive center. New York City was such a center in the early part of the 20th century, however. With seemingly boundless financial resources, a preeminent port and craftsmen from related industries ready to embrace the new technology, it was natural that New York would see its share of

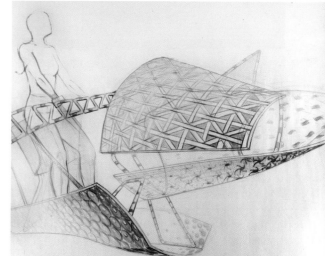

Pratt continues to be the hub of instruction for a plethora of designers in many industries. Left: Pratt Library, today. Above: Study is broad at Pratt and includes learning convexity and how shape and space relates to utility.

Cioppa who has designed government buildings and corporate headquarters, and Carlos Zapata whose firm redesigned Soldier Field in Chicago. Industrial designers Read and Tucker Viemeister, Richard Gioscia of Palm, Charles Pollack and Bruce Hannah of furniture designer Knoll International and packaging designer Marc Rosen. Interior designer Naomi Leff, who designed the flagship Ralph Lauren store in New

Boyer was head of the team at Ford that designed the original 1955 Thunderbird. John Cafaro at General Motors was the chief designer of the Corvette C5, and is currently director of GM's Full Size Truck studio. Michael Santoro led the team that designed the Chrysler Cirrus and Dodge Stratus that enabled the automaker to compete with its Japanese rivals in the

automobile manufacturing. Simplex was known as the automobile "Made in New York City." The Steinway piano company built Mercedes-Benzes in New York City under license.

Coachbuilders were one of the many resources that attracted automobile manufacturing to New York. The oldest was Brewster (see *Automobile Quarterly* Vol.

Read Viemeister was one of Pratt's most interesting graduates. He left his fingerprints on the 1948 Tucker (above, its rendering opposite page). Below: Among the prominent New York coachbuilders of the '20s and '30s was Rollston, which bodied this 1932 Duesenberg J.

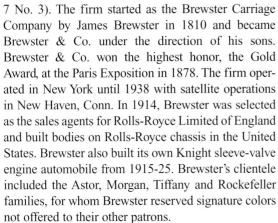

7 No. 3). The firm started as the Brewster Carriage Company by James Brewster in 1810 and became Brewster & Co. under the direction of his sons. Brewster & Co. won the highest honor, the Gold Award, at the Paris Exposition in 1878. The firm operated in New York until 1938 with satellite operations in New Haven, Conn. In 1914, Brewster was selected as the sales agents for Rolls-Royce Limited of England and built bodies on Rolls-Royce chassis in the United States. Brewster also built its own Knight sleeve-valve engine automobile from 1915-25. Brewster's clientele included the Astor, Morgan, Tiffany and Rockefeller families, for whom Brewster reserved signature colors not offered to their other patrons.

Many of the leading early automotive coachbuilders learned their craft at Brewster and other New York firms before entering the nascent automobile industry. James Way designed Pierce-Arrow's cast aluminum bodies from 1904-1920 and Henry Crecelius left Brewster at Edsel Ford's urging to head Lincoln's coachbuilding business. Raymond Dietrich founded LeBaron, and Harry Lonschein created Rollston.

Proliferate designer Richard Arbib was another Pratt alum that went on to shape a wide range of automobiles. Samples here include conceptual renderings for a 1954 Nash Palomino (above right) and a 1940 Buick Riviera (below).

Even those cars not created in New York were often presented in New York first. General Motors hosted salons in New York each year beginning in 1928. The first was held at the Astor Hotel, and then moved to the new Waldorf-Astoria the following year. David W. Temple, author of *GM's Motorama*, described these early events as industrial luncheons, "invitation-only events (that) showcased the products against a backdrop of Persian rugs and landscape paintings."

General Motors continued its private New York product previews until the beginning of WWII. General Motors, Ford and Chrysler Corporation all presented automotive displays to an excited public at the 1939-40 New York World's Fair, which celebrated the coming second half of the century with exhibits like GM's Futurama.

But it was really after WWII that General Motors invited the public to meet it in New York. GM presented its all-new postwar designs at the Waldorf-Astoria in January 1949 before repeating the presentation in Detroit three months later. The show, called

Transportation Unlimited, showed the Buick Riviera hardtop prior to its introduction and prototypes of the Chevrolet Bel Air, Pontiac Catalina and the Cadillac Coupe de Ville, as well as three Cadillac concept cars. In 1953, GM's show was back in the Big Apple and called Motorama. Motorama was an extravaganza that introduced America to dream cars in the bright lights of New York City. A cast of 1,000 people was required to produce, stage and present Motorama, which included elaborate New York-style stage shows in addition to presenting a new batch of GM dream cars each year according to Temple. One hundred twenty-five trucks were required just to ship everything to New York.

GM's Motorama continued from 1953-61 and included appearances in Miami, Los Angeles, San Francisco, Boston and other cities, but only after the show opened in New York in January of each year.

Automakers also topped New York's skyline. The iconic art deco-style Chrysler Building on the corner of Lexington Avenue and 42nd Street, designed by Pratt-trained architect William van Allen and built between 1928 and 1930, was built to be the tallest building in the world with its chrome-nickel steel crescent-shaped spire and stylized ornamentation representing hubcaps, fenders and hood ornaments. In 1964, General Motors began construction of a corporate headquarters on Fifth Avenue, located directly across the street from the Plaza Hotel. The Savoy-Plaza Hotel designed and built in 1927 by the famed architectural firm of McKim, Mead & White, previously occupied the site. The 50-story white-marble and black-glass General Motors Building towers over the southeast corner of Central Park and today houses commercial office space.

SCHOOL OF ART AND DESIGN

New York City was already acknowledged as the creative center of America when Pratt Institute opened its doors to the first 12 students in 1887.

The School of Art and Design proudly points out that "the first art teacher at Pratt was a pupil

Scenes from the Industrial Design Department (left) and the library (right). Opposite: Products from the color and industrial design studios.

of Cezanne; the second was a student of Matisse." Charles Pratt's vision for his school was to "revolutionize education by challenging the traditional concept of education as a purely intellectual exercise." He created a school "where applied knowledge was emphasized and specific skills were taught to meet the needs of a growing industrial economy."

Pratt's philosophy has always placed the institution at the forefront of design education. In 1888, Pratt's "women's department" was among the first to prepare women to work as professionals. Pratt expanded its curriculum in 1938 to grant its first four-year bachelor's degree. Pratt was also the first design school in the United States to require a foundation year for all art students. Pratt's faculty is made up of successful

working professionals in the fields they teach.

Today, Pratt's School of Art and Design offers undergraduate degree programs in Art and Design Education, Art History, Communications Design, Critical and Visual Arts, Digital Arts, Fashion, Fine Arts, Industrial Design, Interior Design, Media Arts and Writing for Publication, Performance and Media, as well as graduate programs in most of these fields. Other undergraduate and graduate degree programs are offered in the School of Architecture.

Students applying to Pratt must complete an application, take the SAT or ACT test and submit a portfolio for review. The portfolio is required to include pencil or charcoal drawings and several examples of two- and three-dimensional work. Pratt's entrance requirements

ing the person for whom the vehicle will be designed. Their designs include a complete exterior and interior. This is where students develop and solidify the skills that will take them into the workplace.

All Pratt students make a formal presentation of their work at the end of every semester. Graduating seniors in Transportation Design and other tracks also display their presentations at a major show in New York City.

A recent endowment to Pratt Institute has enabled the School of Art and Design to consolidate all applied arts in one Design Center, including Industrial Design, Graphic Design, Fashion and Interior Design. "The gift has allowed us to combine all of these departments into one place, and will allow our students to share classes, resources and exposure to other ideas," said Martin Skalski, who teaches Transportation Design. "We already have one Transportation Design class where about 30 percent of the assignment is to design accessories and fashions for the person who the vehicle

is being designed for – the appearance, the style, how does that fit the intended user?" The Design Center also consolidates resources such as a materials library, model-making shops, spray booths, a 2-D printing and output lab, and a 3-D stereo lithography printer enabling students to transfer 3-D designs onto paper.

The cost of an education at Pratt is not insignificant. Tuition is currently approximately $30,000 per year. Books and supplies add another $3,000 per year, depending on programs. An estimated 90 percent of first-year students and half of all Pratt students live on campus, with a typical cost of $6,000 per year and another $3,000 per year for meal plans. Financial aid

are high; however, extraordinary talent may sometimes offset a lower grade point average.

Transportation Design is one of six studio paths students can choose for an Industrial Design major. All Pratt students take the first-year Foundation program. Students who wish to pursue the Industrial Design major are reviewed at the end of the first year before being accepted by the department. The second year continues a survey of art as well as the history of design, drawing and introduction to prototypes. Students begin to explore design on a broader basis.

The third and fourth years emphasize studio work including CAID (computer-aided industrial design) and Alias, and are when industrial design students identify and begin to concentrate on their professional interests. Juniors select a design track that creates a bridge between the first two years and their specialization in the fifth semester, and then work on more functional projects in the sixth semester, including symmetrical, four-wheeled vehicle designs for the first time. Seniors spend an entire year on one project to create a real-world vehicle. They start by research-

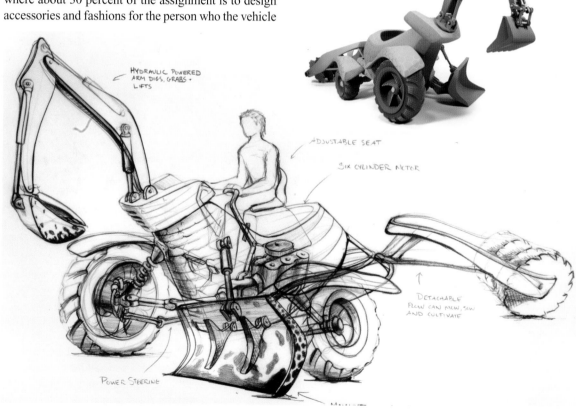

Pratt students are encouraged to experiment with their designs. Shown here is work using the latest in CAID software. Below: Rowena Reed Kostellow founded the Industrial Design Department, where she taught for 50 years. She would become one of the most recognizable names in the industrial design industry.

is available. In spite of the academic and financial requirements, Pratt selects less than 15 percent of applicants each year.

MAKE IT BEAUTIFUL

Rowena Reed Kostellow embodied the essence of the Pratt educational experience. She helped to found the Industrial Design Department at Pratt Institute, where she taught for 50 years and became one of the best-known names in the industrial design profession.

Rowena Reed was born in Kansas City, Mo., in 1900. She enrolled at the University of Missouri in 1918 to study art. But there, she said, "They weren't teaching me anything. There was no order, no organization, no continuity, nothing you could build on." She worked briefly as a journalist and a fashion illustrator before enrolling at the Kansas City Art Institute in 1922, where she met Alexander Kostellow. Kostellow, considered by many to be the father of American industrial design education, became her husband and mentor. In 1929 the couple moved to Pittsburgh where Kostellow had been hired to teach at the Carnegie Technical Institute.

Industrial design was an emerging field in the 1920s, "a facet of industrial art which sought better answers to how objects should look and perform in human hands" in the words of Philip S. Egan, an early practitioner who

also worked with Read Viemeister on the Lippincott Tucker design team. Among those who established the field of industrial design in the United States were Walter Dorwin Teague, Raymond Loewy, Henry Dreyfuss, Norman Bel Geddes and Donald Dohner.

Dohner also taught at Carnegie Tech. Together, Alexander Kostellow and Donald Dohner persuaded the Carnegie Tech administration to establish the first degree-granting program in industrial design in America. In 1934, Dohner was offered an opportunity by Dean James Boudreau of Pratt Institute to establish a department of industrial design at Pratt. Kostellow and Reed accompanied Dohner to New York. Arthur Pulos wrote, "with Alexander Kostellow representing the philosophical, Rowena Reed the aesthetic, and Dohner the practical, they laid the triangular foundation for Pratt's program in industrial design."

Following Rowena Reed's death in 1988, a group of former students gathered together and talked about completing a book describing Reed's educational principals. The group included Louis Nelson, who worked as Reed's assistant when he was a graduate student at Pratt and is the husband of singer Judy Collins. Others in the group included Jim Fulton, Bruce Hannah, Harvey Bernstein, Tucker Viemeister, Lenny Bacich, Jeff Kapec and Lisa Smith. Fulton suggested that the

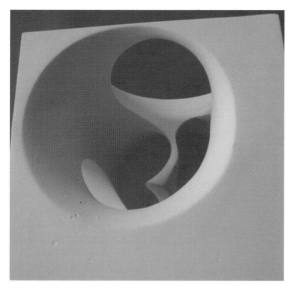

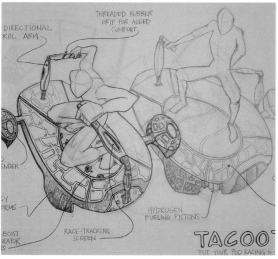

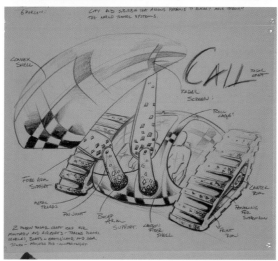

Many disciplines come together in students' work. Common among them all is the Foundation course, for which the painting studio (top right) is utilized.

FOUNDATION

Gail Hannah quotes Alexander Kostellow as writing, like Reed, "My own experiences as an art student had not been too happy, because of the rather haphazard way one had to acquire the necessary knowledge and experience." Together, Reed and Kostellow "pursued their interest in developing a structured language for understanding and teaching visual arts. Their first accomplishment was the development of a curriculum of study for all first-year students in the art school. It was called, appropriately, 'Foundation'."

Foundation "grew out of Kostellow's own experiences with pictorial structure ... and out of Reed's experiments with visual organization in three dimensions." Foundation is described as a year of exploration and study in the fundamentals of art and design. "This vocabulary, which provides the foundation, gives the student a basis which they can retain. That's what education is."

The objective of Foundation is to develop and expand students' "visual thinking." The core curriculum helps students evaluate their previous art experience and exposes them to new ideas and techniques.

group start a foundation, the Rowena Reed Kostellow Fund, to perpetuate her standards of design and education and to help Pratt and all design students in their quest to make things beautiful.

Nelson became chair of the fund and asked Gail Greet Hannah to write the book *Elements of Design*. The book is a tribute to Rowena Reed and a tutorial for those who have come after her. In an introduc-

tion written by Judy Collins, she described her friend Rowena Reed as a "teacher and mentor of some of the most successful industrial designers in the world today. It was as if her very person contained the essence of what she taught – the basis of fine art, architecture, and graphic and industrial design. 'Make it beautiful,' she said, and she was."

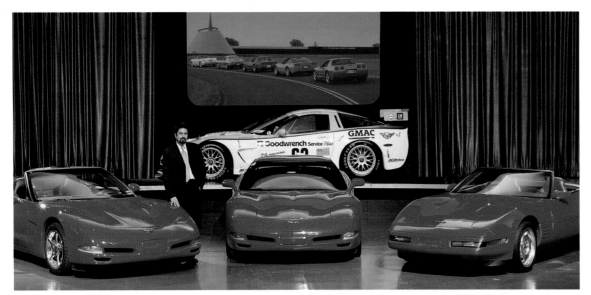

After graduating from Pratt, John Cafaro (above) went to work for General Motors, became the chief designer of the Corvette C5, and is currently director of GM's Full Size Truck studio.

hand and my mind. I don't think about it all the time. I just do it."

DESIGNING FOR THE REAL WORLD

Approximately 200 undergraduate students and 120 graduate students at Pratt choose the industrial design track. Fifteen to 20 specialize in transportation design each year. "We are training generalists," Burger said. Unlike some design schools, students are encouraged to explore different areas and disciplines. Changing majors is common. John Cafaro of GM studied as a product designer with a passion for automobiles. Other Industrial Design graduates design shoes in New York's fashion industry. Michael Santoro

The courses include a fine arts seminar, design history, 2-D drawing and 3-D design, which explores natural forms, and the study of color and composition. One of the most intriguing elements is the study of convexity and concavity.

Skalski has taught at Pratt since 1991. He is currently the driving force behind transportation studies at Pratt, working with Matthew Burger, chair of the Industrial Design Department. "These are pure aesthetic exercises," Skalski said. "This is us. This is who we are." The convexity problem, he explains, is about external surfaces and how they relate. The concavity problem deals with the aesthetics of the negative space, the interior spaces. Nothing in the studio looks remotely like an automobile, or any man-made object. They aren't intended to. "These problems provide visual training tools," he says. "The students have to learn to make decisions looking in three dimensions."

With an understanding of the educational purpose, the abstract shapes begin to reveal themselves as the elements of design. Lisa Smith, executive director of the Rowena Reed Kostellow Fund and a former student, described how "the exercises developed my

Pratt grad Jim Quinlan was responsible for the impressive design found in Ford Thunderbird interiors. Above is the inside of a 1966 Thunderbird. Right: Look for 2007 graduate Alexandra Dymowska to be at the cutting edge of automotive design in the near future.

is a former automobile designer at Chrysler who today is president of MacCase in Carlsbad, Calif. MacCase designs premium cases for Apple Macintosh laptop computers and accessories. "It doesn't matter what you do," Santoro said. "It's the same process."

"From the very beginning the education at Pratt has emphasized designing beautiful things in people's lives," Skalski explained. Including automobiles. In the 1940s, '50s and '60s the auto industry hired entire classes from Pratt. And not just for exterior design. Jim Quinlan designed the swooping interiors in Ford Thunderbirds built in the '50s and '60s and became

director of color and trim at Ford before retiring in 1990. "You could get a job anywhere with a Pratt portfolio, because (it was) more professional," Quinlan said. "I was hired by Frank Hershey, who was director of styling for Ford. He said he liked my portfolio, but I didn't have any sketches of cars. He asked, 'Do you like cars?' I answered, 'Yes,' and he said, 'You're hired.'

"Pratt taught us to design in three dimensions. And that was the difference between Pratt and other schools. That's what we had."

And it remains so. Alexandra Dymowska is a recent Pratt graduate just beginning her career in the GM

Color and Trim studio. She echoes the words of earlier Pratt graduates: "My education at Pratt was one of my most formative, enlightening experiences, because of the 3-D design emphasis." Dymowska completed her undergraduate education at Columbia College in Chicago in fine art painting and sculpture, and then spent three years in the graduate program at Pratt on a fellowship. "One of the most wonderful things at Pratt is learning by doing. You train your hands. Train your eye. It's a cognitive approach. It's really about developing a method of working."

She is also a product of Martin Skalski's innovative program in color and materials.

"It doesn't cost any more to make interiors more sophisticated," Skalski said. "I think one of our strengths is in color, texture and pattern – the surface qualities. The automakers can do anything with interior surface qualities now and in the very near future they will be able to do anything on the exterior with surface qualities. Most car designers have had little color training and are very nervous (in this area)." Pratt offers a graduate color workshop that is unique. Called Color for 3-D Designers, the course teaches color, texture and hue on three-dimensional objects.

John Cafaro also talked about the influence of Pratt designers at GM. "Successful designers at GM for four decades have come from Pratt. They've had a real influence on GM designs. Stan Wilan – who hired me at GM – was the head of the Cadillac studio in the '60s, where the 1967 Cadillac Eldorado was created. (That car) is still influencing young designers today. Bill Porter, in the Pontiac studio, designed the great GTOs and the 1970½ Firebird and Trans-Am. Those cars were simple, bold new statements at the time, really steeped in their 3-D design language. Randy Wittine has had an influence on all of the Corvettes from the mid-1970s 'til today."

"Pratt and Art Center have always been the two big schools," Cafaro continued, "and now the global schools are playing a part at GM. But you get a different perspective at Pratt. For one thing, Pratt is an East Coast school and that's a different culture. You are a more diverse designer and your influences are more international. Your beliefs are more ingrained; you're more versatile and more committed to strong beliefs. And that helps to carry you through a big corporate culture. Pratt has a way of instilling a passion for uncompromised design."

The challenge of training for a global industry elicits a surprising response at Pratt. "GM is looking at a global approach. But how does Saab keep a regional identity?" Burger asked. "How do we differentiate? How do we make something distinct? How do you better prepare for global vision? I think design will (always) be a tool for that."

DESIGNING FOR THE FUTURE

At Pratt, students are taught to find a completely new solution. Classes like Introduction to Transportation Design place an emphasis on drawing, but not drawing something you know. The lesson is to explain the process, new ways and new behavior. Later, students will design a product. It could

Producing novel designs is nothing new at Pratt; experimental approaches often lead to eye-catching style.

be a car. Students are taught to design for the person who will use the product.

"The most important considerations are behavior, style and function," explained Skalski, who teaches the class. "The best way to approach a new stylistic or functional idea is to start with a clear head, not with something that exists. (Instead) the process starts to suggest uses. As it develops more, the use becomes more apparent and the shape becomes something completely new. It's similar to basic research, where scientists might combine different chemicals just to see what happens."

The futuristic designs of Pratt graduates Richard Arbib and Read Viemeister include examples of the extent to which postwar automotive designers could be preoccupied with aircraft and rocket shapes and details. Arbib's 1956 Metropolitan Astra – featured on the cover of *Newsweek* magazine – demonstrates the absurdity of the era, although the front fenders accurately predict the 1963 Buick Riviera.

The principle of designing for the future is sometimes difficult to grasp. The success of the design depends upon its ability to satisfy the style, the behavior and the needs of a population. But what will the buyer want by the time the design reaches the market? It is part of the designer's challenge to "lead" the buyer, to somehow challenge the buyer to accept

something new at precisely the time the buyer might be ready to adapt to a new idea. Nowhere is this truer than with automotive styling. Reach too far – as with the Chrysler Airflow design of the 1930s – and the buyer will reject the product. Design too conservatively – like the recent Ford 500 – and the product runs the risk of looking too bland.

"The best way to initiate truly new designs is to start a design with no preconceptions and no criteria for the design," Skalski said. "A designer could make random marks on a paper or make abstract three-dimensional sculptural statements and then look for suggested new ideas and uses. Using an infinite number of different approaches a designer can find new styles, new ways of doing things and new functions."

Molly McGee's Dergo (p.61) is a design study of a multifunctional machine designed to assist in the development and maintenance of a small farm. The Dergo is described as an example of the outcome of the Pratt design process that develops a purely abstract form into an advanced, functional product for the evolving tastes of society. Color, pattern and texture enhance the form while adding visual interest.

Pratt students also participate in design exercises to adapt new design solutions to needs, as people will perceive them in the future. The TAXI 07 project was sponsored by the Design Trust for Public Space in New York City. Various designers, consultants, manufacturers and design schools, including Pratt Institute, collaborated on innovative design solutions for New York taxis. Eight prototype taxis and related displays

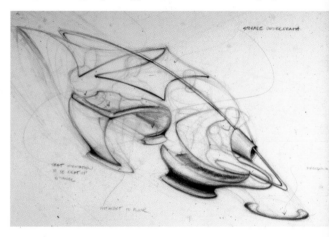

illustrated "innovations in sustainable mobility, accessibility and good design."

Pratt Continuing and Professional Studies offers a pre-college program that immerses students in a four-week summer program on campus modeled after the Pratt undergraduate program. And the Pratt Design Corps offers junior and senior students an opportunity to provide pro-bono design work for non-profit organizations in the community.

The shapes, noises and visions of the future are never far from the Pratt campus. And the beginning of a completely new idea is never far from the mind of a Pratt designer. ◭◲

PATHFINDER
THE LAST REAL RILEY

When the Riley Pathfinder was announced at the 1953 Earls Court motor show it promised a whole new world of "Magnificent Motoring" – it was large, powerful, had advanced styling, was comfortably equipped and was potentially fast. It was also flawed, although only a few insiders were aware of that at the time.

BY GAVIN FARMER

A New Beginning

It was to be the car that Riley enthusiasts consider to be the last real Riley. Dyed-in-the-wool Riley fans have little time for it, however, and will tell you the Harry Rush-designed coach-built RM series was the end of the line as far as true Rileys were concerned.

Whatever your position in the debate, there is little doubt that anything that followed the RMH Pathfinder was little more than a badge-engineered BMC clone, definitely not a Nuffield design, and an automobile that did little to enhance the famous sporting Riley tradition. The Pathfinder was one of those rare cars from the automobile industry insofar as it was a design conceived from the beginning by one man, in this case Gerald Palmer.

When Palmer returned "home" to Nuffield from Jowett (see *Automobile Quarterly* Vol. 42 No. 4) in July 1949, he was appointed chief designer for all future MG and Riley saloons by his colleague A.V. ("Vic")

Oak and was also welcomed back by the company's deputy managing director, Reg Hanks. Responsibility for future Wolseleys was added to his portfolio a little later. These were pre-merger days, although by the time the cars were ready for production a merger between the two giants of the British motor industry – the Nuffield Group (Morris, Wolseley, Riley, MG) and Austin – was a *fait accompli.*

Oak virtually gave Palmer a free hand to design and develop the new range of Wolseley, MG and Riley cars, the only restrictions being that he had to use standard off-the-shelf hardware like engines, gearboxes and rear axles. There would be no absolutely free hand, however, as he enjoyed with the Jowett Javelin. This was Nuffield, a company never noted for its adventurism but well known for its parsimony.

Palmer assembled a small team – believed to have been no more than 10 people – that included Bob Shirley who was in charge of the drawing office, Tom Honeyset, Jim O'Neill and Terry Mitchell to design and develop the Pathfinder and its twin, the Wolseley 6/90.

In correspondence with the author in the 1980s, Palmer remembered: "After some thought and considering the need to use standard components wherever possible, it was obvious to me that four completely new body shells would not be financially viable. Therefore, I decided to design two bodies – a four-seater and a six-seater – and use trim and other means to differentiate between them and maintain the character of each marque."

In the event, the four-seater would carry Wolseley and MG badges, the six-seater Wolseley and Riley badges. Within the Morris drawing office the smaller of the two bodies was given priority, with the result that the Wolseley 4/44 appeared on the market in November 1952 with the MG XPAG 1¼-liter ohv engine, under the hood, although it was engineered to accept the new BMC B-series 1½-liter, four-cylinder engine, which it did in late 1953. The MG Magnette, released in September 1953, was powered by a 60bhp twin-carburetor version of the same B-series engine from the very beginning. Both models were sales suc-

Dave Rowland's well-kept everyday means of transport is this 1956 Riley Pathfinder saloon. It has traveled more than 300,000 miles on its original engine and apart from new pistons and a decoke at 200,000 miles has been completely reliable.

what I had in mind. They were so impressed that the potential volumes they believed they could sell determined the way I would engineer the big Riley and Wolseley body and that it would be made totally in pressed steel."

Years later Palmer cited Mr. Weine, the Swiss importer of Rileys, as the man who influenced him the most insofar as the overall size and concept of the future. There had been talk within Nuffield of the future Riley being a Jaguar competitor, a fact confirmed by Palmer and Weine, although some early thoughts had suggested a close-coupled four-seater in the mold of the old RMF 2½ Litre.

These discussions settled the physical size of the Riley. As it happened, it was about the same size as the RMF saloon with a wheelbase of 9 ft 5½ in, overall length of 15 ft 3½ in, width 5 ft 6 in, height 4 ft 11½ in with front wheel track set at 4 ft 6 in and rear at 4 ft

adamant that any future Riley saloon should feature the famous 2½-liter "Big Four" twin underhead camshaft engine, separate chassis, torsion bar front suspension, rack-and-pinion steering and a torque tube drive arrangement. Where the Wolseley was concerned, early thoughts were to carry over the 6/80's existing 2.2-liter six-cylinder engine with its single chain-driven overhead camshaft and complex valve gear. Like the RM series' Rileys, the 6/80 Wolseley featured longitudinal torsion bars for its independent front suspension.

During late 1951 Vic Oak came to Palmer and advised him that the merger with Austin was definitely on this time – there had been one or two false starts during the previous year – and that Palmer would need to make provision for engines other than the existing Riley and Wolseley units. Palmer again: "That actually did not cause much of a problem because I'd already allowed considerable room in the engine bay. You see,

Above left: Gerald Palmer, English design engineer and creator of the Riley Pathfinder. Above left and right: Palmer claimed the elegant shape of this Bentley coupe by Italian coachbuilder Farina was his inspiration for the Pathfinder's smooth lines.

cesses and both are fondly appreciated today as superb examples of their genre.

It was the larger of the two ranges that was far more interesting and, in many ways, more controversial. Palmer was able to concentrate on the larger models beginning in late 1950. He said of these cars, "I was given virtually no guidance from the board, Hanks or Oak, on the six-seater cars. Obviously their production volume would be considerably less than for the four-seaters so I was unsure as to how I should proceed. That was resolved when I showed some influential dealers, especially London main dealer Jimmy James,

6½ in. Weight with 13 Imperial gallons of fuel in the tank was quoted as 30½ cwt (3,500 pounds).

Palmer experienced some pressure from another quarter: influential Riley enthusiasts and two colleagues, Jack Tatlow and Arnold Farrar. They were

the Riley engine was quite wide and the Wolseley quite tall so any Austin engine would fit. As it eventuated, the big six-cylinder Austin engine (the C-series as they called it) was much bulkier than I'd expected even though it was a completely new design."

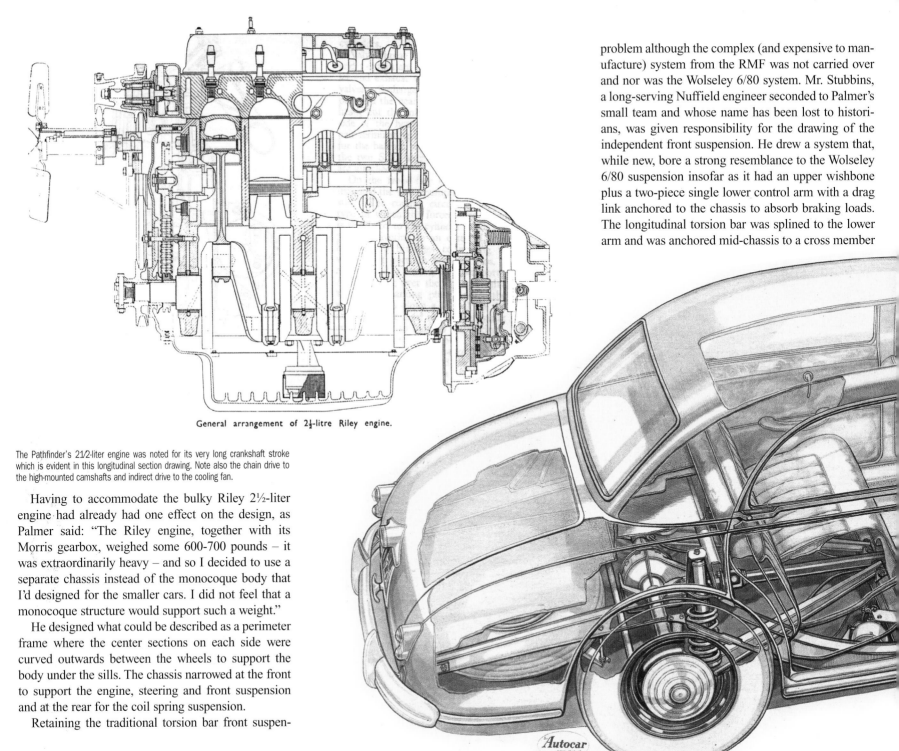

General arrangement of 2½-litre Riley engine.

The Pathfinder's 2½-liter engine was noted for its very long crankshaft stroke which is evident in this longitudinal section drawing. Note also the chain drive to the high-mounted camshafts and indirect drive to the cooling fan.

problem although the complex (and expensive to man-ufacture) system from the RMF was not carried over and nor was the Wolseley 6/80 system. Mr. Stubbins, a long-serving Nuffield engineer seconded to Palmer's small team and whose name has been lost to histori-ans, was given responsibility for the drawing of the independent front suspension. He drew a system that, while new, bore a strong resemblance to the Wolseley 6/80 suspension insofar as it had an upper wishbone plus a two-piece single lower control arm with a drag link anchored to the chassis to absorb braking loads. The longitudinal torsion bar was splined to the lower arm and was anchored mid-chassis to a cross member

Having to accommodate the bulky Riley 2½-liter engine had already had one effect on the design, as Palmer said: "The Riley engine, together with its Morris gearbox, weighed some 600-700 pounds – it was extraordinarily heavy – and so I decided to use a separate chassis instead of the monocoque body that I'd designed for the smaller cars. I did not feel that a monocoque structure would support such a weight."

He designed what could be described as a perimeter frame where the center sections on each side were curved outwards between the wheels to support the body under the sills. The chassis narrowed at the front to support the engine, steering and front suspension and at the rear for the coil spring suspension.

Retaining the traditional torsion bar front suspen-

that also supported the gearbox extension housing. A neat touch was the use of telescopic hydraulic dampers with finned casings to help keep the oil inside cool.

Palmer conceived the rear suspension and former MG chief chassis engineer Terry Mitchell was responsible for the detailed engineering drawings of it. When interviewed for an article published in *Thoroughbred and Classic Cars*, April 1992, Mitchell said, "My rear suspension used a beam axle, radius arms, coil springs, Panhard rod and telescopic dampers fitted to a perimeter frame. One day Vic Oak, who was engineering director, came around, looked at my drawing board with the layout showing the location for the Panhard rod and said, 'That bracket will break, you know.' But rather than suggest a modification he just walked on. So it went into production and they did break until a modification was made."

Palmer disliked leaf springs intensely which was why the larger cars dispensed with them. "They were crude hang-overs from the horse and cart days; the inter-leaf friction brought with it a degree of harshness to the ride that I felt was unacceptable and compromised the handling, something that was completely absent from a coil spring," he mentioned to the author. "Besides, I designed the suspension with a level of refinement that had never been achieved at Nuffield previously."

As English historian Jon Pressnell wrote in *Classic and Sportscar* in October 1985, "This unusual and

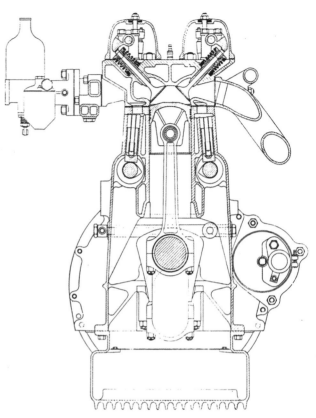

Cross section of 2½-litre Riley engine

advanced layout met the spirit of the Riley men's stipulations on rear axle location, it not being possible to follow them to the letter as the BMC rear axle could not accept a torque tube."

Palmer was inspired by outside design influences when he came to pen the lines of the four-seater and six-seater bodies. On this occasion it was the Battista "Pinin" Farina body that he saw at the 1948 Paris Motor Show on a Bentley Mark VI chassis. "I thought it was the most elegant design I had ever seen," Palmer said.

The body styling that Palmer developed for the future Riley Pathfinder (and Wolseley 6/90) was characterized by the smooth curves of the panels running back from the traditional upright grille (with radiator "cap") from where they sloped gently back and

Above: The general layout of the Pathfinder was in line with contemporary ideas of the fifties. Unusual, however, was the unique rear suspension design and the gearshift lever on the driver's right. Top: Apart from its long stroke, the Riley 2½-liter engine was famous for its valve gear that provided a hemispherical combustion chamber with the spark plug centrally positioned.

down to the chromed rear bumper. The body sides were completely unadorned, lacking swage lines or decoration, at least initially, and the door handles were cleverly styled into the discreet chrome trim at waist level. Palmer's designs were among the first in England to embrace the so-called "Ponton" look that was then sweeping the styling studios of the rest of the automobile world.

A full-size mock-up of the Pathfinder was completed by late 1950 and displayed on the turntable in the Nuffield styling studios wearing the fake registration RLY 999, its Cowley Drawing Office project number. Notable on the mock-up was the use of a split-vee windshield, quarter lights in the front doors

Left and above: Riley sales catalogs were always beautifully illustrated works of art. The catalog on the right was for the Two-Point-Six, which was really a Wolseley 6/90 clone. Below: Pathfinders did occasionally make competition appearances, usually in rallies but sometimes on race circuits; here H. Grace is at Oulton Park in 1957.

The Riley engine has been developed from a long and highly successful motor racing experience. It is a notably compact unit yet delivers tremendous power. Specially tuned, these engines have won, within their classification, every race of importance and have achieved a remarkable series of successes in Monte Carlo Rallies, Alpine Trials, and the most gruelling competitive events all over the world.

and narrow horizontal egg-crate grilles either side of the traditional Riley grille. All would be changed for production. A year later a definitive mock-up was completed and presented and signed off for production; it differed only in minor details from the original: a one-piece curved windshield and tidied-up front grilles with integrated fog lights.

Riley enthusiasts had demanded a traditional interior. This of course meant leather upholstery and lashings of walnut trimming on the dashboard and door cappings. The instruments – three large-diameter, round Smiths gauges – were grouped together as a unit in front of the driver, a first for a Riley. The center dial was a combination unit with fuel, temperature, amps and oil pressure gauges flanked to the left by the speedometer and on the right by the tachometer. Between the mock-up shown to management and production, the graphics changed and the combination gauge needles all pivoted from the middle rather than from the outside. In the center of the dash was a round radio speaker face with provision for an HMV set below while a deeply recessed glove box was in front of the passenger.

Palmer's original interior had bucket front seats with a center-floor gearshift lever but these, too, would change courtesy of Nuffield management decisions.

Carrying six passengers necessitated that the front seat be of the bench type, and the gearshift was therefore moved to the right of the driver (on right-hand-drive cars) a la Bentley Mark VI. Bucket seats were retained as an option, however, which had no effect on the gearshift position.

As James Taylor wrote in his definitive book *RM-Series Riley*: "With one or two minor changes, the mock-up was approved as the basis for a production vehicle, and the Nuffield management decided to go for pressed-steel construction of its body."

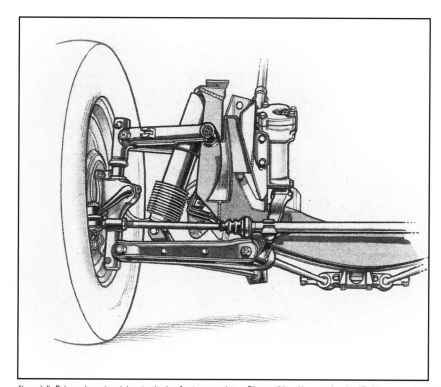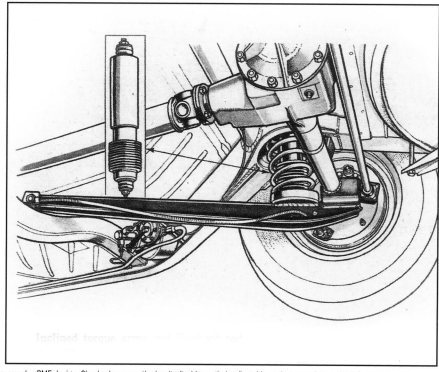

Above left: Palmer chose to retain a torsion-bar front suspension, a Riley tradition. However, he simplified it compared with the complex RMF design. Clearly shown are the longitudinal bars, their adjustable anchorage points and the finned tubular dampers.
Above right: To provide the quality of ride and handling Palmer wanted, he used coil springs at the rear, rare in the fifties. The heavy live axle was located by long trailing arms pivoted mid-body with a transverse Panhard rod. Again note the finned dampers.

Although no records exist today, and Palmer was not sure, Taylor wrote that "photographs show a 1952-registered car, TFC 226, and it would be reasonable to suppose that this was the first prototype." What Palmer did remember, however, was that "it was a very poorly made car that needed an awful lot of development work before it would have been ready for production."

After the first prototype had been built, orders were placed with Fisher and Ludlow in Birmingham for the supply of pressed body panels and John Thompson Motor Pressings in Wolverhampton for the chassis frame. At this time Palmer was approached by Joe Kinchin, chief engineer from Girling, who proceeded to "sell" him on the idea of adopting their new, and as it eventuated unproved, twin trailing shoe design for the front brakes. Palmer was amenable to the idea, although it did mean having to use a vacuum servo to reduce foot pedal pressure to acceptable levels. For

Palmer, the trouble was, the vacuum unit was bulky and there was no way it would fit into the already cramped under-hood space. The solution was to mount it remotely on a chassis cross member adjacent to the right-hand rear wheel where it was unprotected from road grime and its effects. Interestingly, the Wolseley 6/90 retained its Lockheed non-boosted braking system carried over basically unchanged from the 6/80.

In Palmer's mind, the greatest compromise he was forced to make was to dispense with the excellent Riley rack-and-pinion steering system so beloved by owners. It was substituted with the Bishop cam-and-peg system, because he'd had to move the Riley engine forward in the chassis, leaving no clearance under the forthcoming BMC C-series six-cylinder engine for the rack.

With sales of the RMF down to a trickle, the small team at Abingdon was pressured by the new BMC

management to display a Pathfinder at the 1953 Earls Court motor show (a non-runner) held in October where it generated a great deal of enthusiasm from the media, dealers and public. However, behind the scenes all was not well with the program. With the retirement of Vic Oak from the senior engineering position at Nuffield and John Rix from a similar position at Austin, Palmer was the most senior and experienced engineer remaining in the newly formed British Motor Corporation (BMC). He was no longer in day-to-day management after his promotion to chief engineer of chassis and body for BMC and there were many issues that urgently needed resolution. The major ones were body leaks (of water in Europe, water and dust in Australia and South Africa), the braking system, clutch judder and the steering. Another issue with the suspension would come to light after production had begun.

The Riley Pathfinder was both elegant and fast, with a handsomely styled steering wheel and instrument panel, as well as a more-than-adequate four-cylinder that produced a listed 102 bhp at 4400 rpm.

PRODUCTION, WITH PROBLEMS

Nuffield director S.V. Smith made the decision to push the Pathfinder into production, disregarding the pleas from long-serving MG engineer Cyril Cousins and others who knew it was not ready. Among those was Nuffield chief engineer Charlie Griffin, who drove one of the few cars built out along the Woodstock road and skidded off the road backwards through a hedge – he promptly nicknamed the car "Hedgefinder." He joined Cousins and MG boss John Thornley in voting against immedi-

ate production but all were overruled by the new BMC management.

As it was, following the display in October 1953, customer cars did not begin to roll off the Abingdon lines until December of that year. By mid-1954 barely 200 cars had been completed and delivered to dealers, so slow was the start-up – two to three cars a week in the first months of the year. There was not even a car available to the media.

It was at this time that it was found that the bodies would not properly fit on the chassis supplied by Thompson's without much hammering and modifying. When investigated it was found that the chassis

were being welded on wooden trestles and not on the jigs Palmer had designed and made for the purpose. A corollary of this was the fact that the brackets for locating the rear-suspension Panhard rod were out of alignment, putting added strain on them causing them to break.

Interestingly, in view of what followed, the English press gave the Pathfinder a quite rapturous welcome, such was the affection for Rileys. John Bolster, writing in *Autosport* in the Feb. 18, 1955, edition (a full year after regular production had begun) said after driving the one press car (registered KJB 372) driven by all the magazines: "This is, in fact, an exception-

The Riley Pathfinder interior was a typically English club atmosphere with polished walnut dashboard, a full set of instruments and supple leather upholstery. Just visible are the floor pivoted foot pedals.

ally well-equipped car and one in which the comfort of the occupants has obviously been greatly studied. It is large and luxurious, with no attempt to cut weight, and I expect the makers would be horrified if anybody called it a sports car! Yet, I shall remember it most for that easy 100 mph, that dear little gear lever, and the sure way it held the treacherous roads of winter. This is certainly the best car to bear the name Riley."

Bolster timed the Pathfinder at 101 mph and at 16.5 seconds for the 0-60 sprint, good going for a four-cylinder car that weighed 3,360 pounds. What was important was that it out-performed the fondly remembered old Riley 2½ liter.

The Motor and *Autocar* were no less effusive in their praise of the Pathfinder in their issues of Dec. 8, 1954, and Feb. 25, 1955, respectively.

Smith's decision to force the car into production prematurely had disastrous effects on the dealer body and Riley's Service division at Abingdon. Initially complaints poured in from angry dealers and disillusioned owners who had experienced failure of the braking system, the rear suspension, clutch shudder and water leaks. The Clayton-Dewandre brake booster was a unit that needed constant maintenance (a fact not

Compared with many other British designs from the early '50s, the Riley Pathfinder's styling was in line with contemporary work from its European rivals.

fully understood by Service), otherwise it would fail and when this happened its default position was to lock the brakes fully, making the Pathfinder immovable. This problem remained with the car for its production life, although once Girling and Riley Service came to grips with its characteristics (from 1955 production) it ceased to be a major issue. Incidentally it was a problem for Jaguar who also used the same braking system but the media, especially later classic car writers, unfairly concentrated their vitriol on the Riley.

Even as late as 1964 BMC was issuing service bulletins to its dealers because it was aware that many owners had unnecessarily spent hundreds of pounds on work on the Girling system. As Riley Pathfinder expert David Rowlands commented, "BMC kept messing about changing brake system components right through to 1957 … entirely pointless and an enormous waste of time, effort and money."

The rear suspension issue was really solved once the correct manufacturing process was instigated, but as a precaution from autumn 1955, a second Panhard rod that crossed over and behind the existing rod was fitted, a situation that remained until the Wolseley rear suspension was fitted later. However, as Rowlands said, "The safety of Palmer and Mitchell's live coil spring rear axle has been proven over the past 50 years of continuous use by many, many owners. That second tie bar was really superfluous. And the securing bolt was fine and rarely gave trouble once the alignment of the Panhard rod was correct – another myth debunked."

As for the body leaks, the then head of Riley's Technical Services department, Tony Day, told author James Taylor: "Fishers were not good pressers. They could never manage to produce a panel without spring-back, so there was always fitting problems that incidentally disappeared when the pressed steel-made Wolseley body was adopted for the Two-Point-Six."

From the moment the Pathfinder went into production, the engineers at Abingdon instigated myriad changes in an effort to build a car that would be reliable and enjoyable for its owner. Late in 1954 came the first upgrades: the front torsion bars were softened to counter the harsh ride complaints; the steering ratio was lowered to take some of the effort out of it together with wider section tires (6.70x16 in place of 6.00x16); quarter vent windows were added in lieu of draft deflectors; single-speed wipers replaced the two-speed originals; and the chrome strips on top of the front fenders were eliminated as were the strips along the hood edges.

The original Morris manual gearbox was replaced by the BMC C-type unit in 1955. It was still a four-speed unit with a non-synchromesh first gear, bringing with it hydraulic clutch operation that removed much of the shudder problem. A new C-type rear axle was taken from the Wolseley 6/90 as part of a rationalization program. By late 1956 with availability of the C-type box problematic, the Austin-Healey and Westminster gearboxes found their way into the Pathfinder. Four different manual gearboxes in four years!

So many historians want to denigrate the Pathfinder and, while it is true that it sold in small numbers and was troublesome, they seem to have lost sight of the fact that Rileys were always niche models; they were never mass-sellers. They appealed to a select group of people for whom being an individual was more impor-

tant than whether their car enjoyed the latest in styling. Riley people tended to be hard drivers who demanded a lot from their cars and were very vocal when things went wrong. Unfortunately, far too many things went wrong with the early (1954 production) Pathfinders, a fact not made any more palatable by the fact that the engineers working on the car knew in their hearts that it was foolhardy to have produced the car when it was nowhere near ready. Palmer himself knew it needed considerable further development, but he was too gentle and refined a man to stand toe-to-toe and cuss with Leonard Lord over engineering detail and soon was disillusioned.

SIZING UP THE COMPETITION

When introduced in 1953, the Pathfinder was priced at the not inconsiderable £1382 (approx. $3,870) that made the Jaguar Mk VII a price competitor even though that car had a dohc 3.4-liter six-cylinder engine. The later Jaguar Mk I 2.4 was a similar price but with superior performance and reputation. And the Rootes Group was fielding its Sunbeam-Talbot 90 and Humber Hawk saloons, both powered by big 2¼-liter four-cylinder engines, the 90 being a sporting saloon in much the same vein as the Riley.

From the mass-produced end of the market, Ford was marketing its excellent Zephyr Six with similarly slab-sided styling and with a spirited, smooth and completely new six-cylinder engine under the hood. It cost a mere £754 (approx. $2,110). Even BMC entered the family saloon market with the Wolseley 6/90 and the Austin Westminster powered by the same 2.6-liter engine. and Both were several hundred pounds less expensive.

Timing is an essential ingredient in any commercial success and here the Pathfinder was crippled with a double whammy. While it was conceived by one of the British automobile industry's most talented design engineers, it was a time of great turmoil within the Nuffield group that had concentrated its early postwar efforts on the hugely successful Morris Minor and had

neglected the "rich" end of its corporate model range. Their small design and development team had to contend with the merger and politics of the new regime headed by the autocratic head of BMC, Leonard Lord. Inculcated in that was a disdain for Nuffield people and products.

The Pathfinder was always meant to be a small-volume, premium-priced sporting saloon. Yet the new BMC management seemed unable to grasp that, as they battled with the monumental task of blending the Austin and Morris ranges together and affecting some kind of rationalization within the vast and disorganized conglomerate. For its time it was extremely well equipped with its leather upholstery, polished walnut dashboard and door garnish panels, floor carpeting, heater/demister, trafficators operated from the chromed horn ring on the steering wheel, map-reading light, and in-built fog lights, to list a few of the long list of standard fittings.

Many Riley enthusiasts and owners believe the Pathfinder became a good car from 1955 onwards when its development was taken over by the people at Abingdon and there was less interference from Cowley. The idea of repositioning the Pathfinder upmarket against the Jaguar MK 1 continued. To that end Palmer designed a new double-overhead camshaft cylinder head for the new C-series six, one of which was built and fitted to a prototype coded EX207 – nicknamed Thornley's barge – in the Abingdon system. Disc front brakes were fitted and, though the car went well and all who drove it loved it, it was decided not to proceed. The car was relegated to being a works hack for many years before being broken up. A significant opportunity was lost.

Towards the end of 1955, Palmer resigned from BMC when CEO Leonard Lord used a negative report from The *Autocar* on the Wolseley 6/90 to offer him a sideways promotion. The real reason was that Lord wanted a former colleague of Palmer, Alec Issigonis, to return from Alvis as chief engineer and he needed Palmer out of the way. He went to Vauxhall as a senior engineer and completed his professional career there.

The last Riley Pathfinders were built for the 1957

model year; these inherited the Wolseley 6/90 Mk III chassis as part of a rationalization of parts. This chassis had reverted to semi-elliptic leaf springs for the rear suspension and had a modified chassis rail to accommodate an automatic gearbox. Other changes included duotone paintwork and a revised dash in which the glovebox was no longer recessed.

Sales, however, continued to decline and on Feb. 12, 1957, the last Pathfinder rolled off the Abingdon production line and into history thereby bringing an end to "Magnificent Motoring" that had been a Riley advertising byline for many years.

With the intelligent use of modern materials and technology, all of the Pathfinder's problems can be and have been cured making it one of the most impressive English cars from the '50s. It was fast, supremely comfortable and carried with it a sporting heritage that few cars had at the time. Its handling was more than acceptable although it must be said that the RMF with its rack-and-pinion steering was far sharper than the Pathfinder's cam-and-peg system. In addition, Palmer's superbly innovative coil spring rear suspension system had the dual benefits of an absorbent ride and good roadholding, and its foibles can be easily dealt with.

Jon Pressnell summed the situation up perfectly in *Classic & Sportscar*: "A basically good car, launched at a difficult transitional phase in the history of the British motor industry, the Pathfinder was the victim of imperfect execution and insufficient development. It deserved a better fate." ▱

The Two-Point-Six

B MC management seemingly could not end the name Riley with the demise of the Pathfinder. The name was continued briefly on a saloon badged as the Two-Point-Six that was in reality a Wolseley 6/90 Mk III wearing different badges.

Apart from the loss of the coil spring rear suspension to be replaced with semi-elliptic leaf springs and the discontinuing of the troublesome Clayton-Dewandre Girling braking system to be replaced by the Lockheed system (with remote booster) used on the 6/90, the Two-Point-Six was powered by BMC's new C-series six-cylinder ohv engine. It was tuned to produce 101 bhp at 4750 rpm using twin SU HS4 carburetors – 9 bhp less than the Pathfinder.

Inside, the dashboard had been revised yet again (the third time) with the speedometer and tachometer remaining in front of the driver and the auxiliary gauges now flanking the central radio speaker with the radio itself now placed low down in front of the passenger. A new and larger rear window was fitted, as were hooded headlights, indicator lights under the parking lights, fog lights and a full-length chrome strip that delineated the duotone body colors. Even the (false) radiator cap was gone.

It was a sad end to a motoring epoch, one that many feel was an insult to the famous name.

Pathfinder Time Line

October 1953	Pathfinder introduced at the London Motor Show
October 1954	Central jacking incorporated into car's specifications
October 1955	Chrome body pieces behind the headlights and on the side of hood were replaced by painted coachlines; flush-fitting glovebox; Borg Warner overdrive optional (required a revised chassis)
November 1955	Hydraulic clutch operation
November 1956	Semi-elliptic leaf spring rear suspension; facia revised
February 1957	Pathfinder discontinued
August 1957	Riley Two-Point-Six announced (Wolseley 6/90 clone) with wide rear window, over-rider mounted front fog lights, 2.6-liter C-series six-cylinder ohv engine, 4-speed manual with or without overdrive, Borg Warner 3-speed automatic
May 1959	Riley Two-Point-Six discontinued

RILEY PATHFINDER PRODUCTION*

1954	889**
1955	2,719
1956	1,477
1957	67
Total	5,152

* Figures taken from *RM-Series Rileys*, J. Taylor   ** 1953 production Pathfinder numbers included

RILEY PATHFINDER PRODUCTION BY MARKET TYPE

	Home Market	Export RHD	Export LHD	CKD RHD	Chassis RHD	Total
1954	551	264	74	-	-	889
1955	1,916	638	152	12	1	2,719
1956	1,289	97	83	8	-	1,477
1957	42	17	8	-	-	67
	3,798	1,016	317	20	1	5,152

The Pathfinder was readily identifiable by its traditional upright grille with its blue diamond badge. Owner: Bill Watson.

Pontiac Pack Rat

John McMullen solves his space problem

Many of John McMullen's cars have won awards at shows, and he has many to show. Today you will find more than 50 immaculate examples of early electrics, polished brass-era gems, classics and postwar machines, all of them American.

BY PHIL BERG

Trophies line the floors in front of McMullen's cars. Being a Pontiac dealer, he felt a loyalty to keep a modern Pontiac collection, with prototype Trans Am wagonbacks and rare Fiero GTs. He has a few classic Pontiac pickups and even older Pontiac touring cars. He has an addition to one garage with only electric and steam cars, including an 1899 Columbia electric. "I just sort of took a liking to the electric car because it's very little maintenance … I have more electric cars than anyone in the world right now."

Among the seven garages on his 485-acre farm,

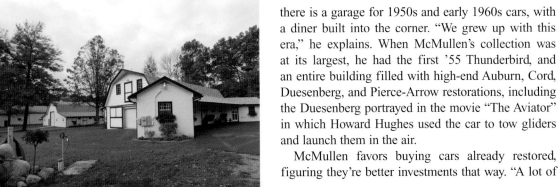

there is a garage for 1950s and early 1960s cars, with a diner built into the corner. "We grew up with this era," he explains. When McMullen's collection was at its largest, he had the first '55 Thunderbird, and an entire building filled with high-end Auburn, Cord, Duesenberg, and Pierce-Arrow restorations, including the Duesenberg portrayed in the movie "The Aviator" in which Howard Hughes used the car to tow gliders and launch them in the air.

McMullen favors buying cars already restored, figuring they're better investments that way. "A lot of

and adoptive parent to pretty much all of America's automotive history. Several times annually car club members have filled McMullen's front-yard parking after traveling on invitation to visit the collections.

His original converted barn contains only antique brass-era cars. When he started his collection, "I

Multiple award-winning 1912 Buick Touring Model 43 50hp landed in another collector's garage for $330,000 last June.

people come in here and tell me more about my cars than I ever thought." His favorite Duesenberg was the one originally owned by comedian Joe E. Brown and then by Howard Hughes. Hughes had the car modified with a large hook on the back to attach tow lines for his gliders, and the rear bodywork of the car had been removed. *Los Angeles Times* owner Otis Chandler bought the car from Hughes, restored it to its original specifications and then took it to the Pebble Beach Concours d'Elegance. Afterwards, McMullen bought the car from Chandler. McMullen has shown five of his own cars at Pebble Beach, as well as other shows around the country. Every car he's shown has won an award.

McMullen had just six cars in 1988. Until last year, he had amassed a collection of 130 cars, meticulously restored and parked in chronological order from the end of the 19th century to the 1970s in the 36,000-

square-foot space of all of his garages.

"I thought it would be nice to have maybe six or seven cars, so I converted this barn 18 years ago," he explains. The McMullen's had moved into a former thoroughbred horse farm, which had a horse barn and a machine shed on the sprawling property. "I built a third building, then I said, 'That's absolutely the last one.' Then you see what happened: I built onto it." But each time he found out about a special car, his instinct to adopt sprang forth. He always reasoned that he had enough acreage to expand his garage village.

So he built a fourth building. Then a fifth, a sixth and, finally, a seventh. Two of the garages gained additions as well. "Each time I said, 'Oh oh, I'm running out of room again,'" he explains. "The thing is, when you find a beautiful car you have got to have a place to put it." The growth happened about every other year, and now, for the past few years, he's been a caretaker

cleaned the barn out and I put my first car in there, which was a 1932 Packard. I never thought I'd have a Packard, but my uncle worked at Packard Motor Car company and he used to drive Packards." McMullen had the car restored, showed it at the Meadow Brook concours in the 1980s, and won a trophy. "That

inspired me to get going. I took it to Pebble Beach and won 'Most Elegant' and also first place. So that got me all excited." His next car was a Cadillac V16, a one-off with a body built by the Mercury coach company. "When it was done, I put it in the barn." Bit by the show bug, McMullen realized that he wasn't going to let a lack of space deter him from acquiring cars he loved.

The collection grew because during the lengthy time period for each of his cars to be restored, he would stumble upon other cars he liked, and buy them. "In the meantime," he explains, "while they were being restored I picked up two or three cars here and there. It's amazing how when you do get interested and you really want to put a collection together, a lot of people will call who have cars."

Despite the rapid growth of his collection, all of the

The hood of a 1913 Packard, which sold for $517,000 at the June auction, frames other cars in the brass building.

cars are in top shape. "I've done so much of it, that after a while you sort of get pickier." All of the cars run. Keeping up the maintenance of 130 cars proved to be a task he couldn't make work on his own. "Fuel pump gaskets, brakes, they all go bad," he says about cars that sit without running for long periods of time. Only one of the seven garages – the working shop – is not carpeted. "Carpeting is civilized," he says, "but I think if I was to do it again I'd probably put some kind of tile down."

Overwhelmed by the task of keeping 130 cars in good running condition, last June McMullen enlisted a couple dozen staff from RM Auctions to cull his collection by about 83 cars and bikes at the pastoral setting of his farm. Before the auction, RM estimated the value of the collection between $7.5 and $10 million. Highlights were a Duesenberg J Tourster that sold for

In between this '37 Cord, which was auctioned of $297,000, and a 1941 Derham-bodied Cadillac Series Sixty Special Town Car once owned by movie actress Bette Davis is a spotless 1933 V-12 Packard Club Sedan.

$1,485,000 at the auction, as well as a V16 Cadillac Murphy-bodied Phaeton that sold for $1,056,000.

The auction was a private, invitation-only event, and took just one day. The toughest part of selling all of these cars presented a challenge: McMullen had only a dozen or so gel cell batteries, which he had kept on chargers in the garages, and installed them in whichever car he felt like driving on any given day.

McMullen originally bought the large horse farm because he likes hunting, not because he wanted to collect cars. "I really bought this place, with no intentions whatsoever of cars, but I just love this space."

"My dad was a mechanic, and I was always helping him with cars," McMullen adds. He began his career, however, as a salesman and opened a Pontiac dealership outside of Detroit in 1966. He then expanded to a second dealership in the city of Pontiac and eventually opened three more dealerships in Florida. "At one time I had seven dealerships and I just felt it was time to shrink down, so I sold all the dealerships with the exception of the first one."

During the June auction, McMullen sold a GTO convertible for $286,000. Once a Pontiac dealer, always a Pontiac dealer. AQ

JOIE RAY
Auto Racing's Jackie Robinson

Nearly six decades before Lewis Hamilton turned the Formula One world on its head, Joie Ray was trying to become the first African-American professional driver in the world.

BY L. SPENCER RIGGS

The caption beside Joie Ray's photo in a high school yearbook read: "Wants to be a race driver." It was perhaps the greatest understatement ever written about the modest native of Louisville, Ky. It would be an uphill battle from the rough and rutted small-town dirt tracks to the quest of all such drivers, the Indianapolis 500. It was a difficult climb for any aspiring young driver in post WWII America. However, unlike his contemporaries, Ray's road would be a little longer and rougher. Joie Ray was African-American.

As a youngster, Ray's first exposure to racing came at the old half-mile dirt track located at the Louisville Fairgrounds. After watching the stalwarts of the day ply their trade – especially a fellow Louisvillian named "Wild Bill" Cantrell – the wide-eyed youngster never thought of being anything but a racer.

"I first saw Bill Cantrell when I was 13 or 14 years old," Ray recalled. "I would definitely consider him one of my heroes."

By the time Ray was old enough to race, the old "Gold and Glory Sweepstakes" circuit – a negro racing league headquartered in Indianapolis and raced throughout the Midwest – had disappeared. The only road open to him was the tough and dangerous "outlaw" circuit. But even on these dust-laden bullrings, few if any black drivers were plying their trade. In reality, Ray would be one of the few black drivers in the world.

After graduating from Central High School, Ray started haunting the pit areas of tracks sanctioned by the Midwest Dirt Track Racing Association (MDTRA) founded by Don Wickliff and Dan Sheeks. The tracks were usually a cut below the standards of the major-league AAA venues. But the racing was exciting, rough-and-tumble competition at its best. And the circuit produced more than 40 drivers who graduated to the Indy 500 ranks.

It was "run what you brung," anything-goes sprint car racing. There were few rules and even fewer safety measures. Crash helmets were mandatory, but many of the contestants didn't even bother to wear a safety belt.

"In that day, on any circuit, the best way to stay in one piece was to keep her right side up and out of the fence," Don Wickliff once said.

With his winning, outgoing personality, Ray quickly made friends around the circuit. His idol Cantrell, future four-time IMCA sprint car champ Bobby Grim, former MDTRA champ Chick Smith and Wickliff were some of his first friends in the sport. Smith soon made the eager, young, black man part of his pit crew, and Ray learned many a track lesson from the veteran driver.

"I remember when Joie first asked me about driving in one of our events," Wickliff said. "I didn't see any reason why he couldn't. After all, he was already an accepted member of our racing scene."

"It was really hard for an up-and-coming white driver to get a decent ride, though," Wickliff continued. "So, I told Joie that maybe he should try and buy his own car, at first."

Then Ray had a stroke of luck. He hit a local, private lottery for a few hundred dollars. After weeks of scanning racing publications for an affordable car, he found a well-used little four-cylinder Dodge-powered sprinter for $450.

Since his funds were limited, and the racer was in Macon, Ga., Ray asked the owner if he would meet

Left: Always grinning, Joie Ray in the No. 69 sprinter awaits the start of an IMCA race in 1949. The tow rope was used to pull-start the cars. Right: Chick Smith was a champion of the MDTRA circuit. He was also a friend of Ray. When Smith lost his life in an accident, Ray rededicated himself to making it to the big time in racing.

the announcer opened the microphone to call the drivers out for warm-up laps, Ray climbed into his car near the judge's stand.

"Hey, what the heck is going on?" blurted the announcer. "Is that n----- gonna drive?"

With that, the area around the announcer suddenly grew dark, as the shadows of the hulking Cantrell and Smith surrounded the offender. Wickliff, the third man coming to Ray's defense, heard some mention of throwing the culprit from the second story window. When the commotion died down, Cantrell and Smith returned to the pit area to assure Ray that things had been put right. When the microphone was keyed a second time, the message was quite different.

"Ladies and gentlemen, in car number seven we have Joie Ray, the world's only colored race driver."

him and bring the car to Franklin, Tenn. With the deal struck, Ray was so excited he forgot to have a trailer hitch installed on his passenger car.

"I got to Franklin on a weekend, and everything was closed," Ray said. "I had to wait until Monday to get a hitch."

Unfortunately, the Dodge sprinter was pretty well used up. But Ray's neighbors Phil and J.B. Montgomery and the ever-present Chick Smith helped ready the car for Ray's first race.

The spring of 1947 was quite a time for black athletes. On Tuesday, April 15, 1947, Jackie Robinson played his first game of major league baseball for the Brooklyn Dodgers, breaking the color barrier in the stick-and-ball sport.

Only nine days previous, on Easter Sunday, April 6, Joie Ray made his debut as a race driver. There were 23 other cars entered at the high-banked, half-mile dirt Mitchell Speedway in Mitchell, Ind. The slowest car in the field was "Joe's Special." When the green flag dropped on the consolation race field (an event for non-money winners and slower cars), Ray thought he was being strafed by a machine gun. The rocks and dirt slammed into his cockpit from every direction. He finished a very distant last in the event and didn't make the main. He began to wonder if he had what it took to

Top: Former driver turned car owner Mel Leighton poses with his Riley-powered sprint car. This is the machine in which Ray (above left) passed his driver's test and competed in his first AAA event. Indy 500 star Jack McGrath drove this car early in his career. Above right: Ray with the Hughes Dreyer-powered sprinter at Salem, Ind., in the early 1950s. Ray would have been the first black driver at Indianapolis had things gone differently.

be a racer. It only took a week for the answer.

The next race was at Franklin, Ind., where the half-mile fairgrounds dirt track was promoted by Wickliff. Amazingly, surrounded by his friends, this was where Ray met with his first taste of racial prejudice around a race track. Wickliff's regular announcer wasn't available, so a substitute was pressed into service. Just as

The words may not have been correct, but the announcer's pattern of oratory would have done any Shakespearean actor proud.

When the announcer was through with Ray's introduction, the usually mild-mannered Wickliff's voice came over the offender's shoulder in a tone that would freeze molten lava. "That's good. But don't ever let me

it was a step up from the underpowered little Dodge. And Ray drove it for all it was worth. He gave a good account of himself in the car, but his mettle was tested several times.

One day at Jungle Park Speedway near Rockville, Ind. – a railless half-mile dirt track with five turns and a perimeter lined with large trees – the Todd sprinter suffered a broken spindle. With the front suspension folded up like so much rope, and Ray clinging to the useless steering wheel, the airborne racer flew between two giant oaks and disappeared into the woods. "I didn't get a scratch," Ray would laugh whenever he told the story. "But it was some ride!"

"After that day at Jungle, I didn't know if I'd done Joe a favor or not," Bobby Grim said. "Todd's old car was pretty rough, but it was amazing what Joe could get out of it. I'd say he did just about as well as I'd done with it."

Since Jungle Park's unyielding bark-covered sentinels had ended the careers of many an established racer, some thought Ray's romp through the woods might change his mind about driving. But the next

Above: In Ray's youth, "Wild Bill" Cantrell was his first racing hero. Cantrell helped Ray during his early career and was a protector of the young, black driver. Below: Three-time IMCA champ Frank Luptow was the king of the outlaw dirt when Ray outwitted him at Wausau. Luptow told Ray to enjoy his win, that there wasn't always enough racing luck to go around.

hear you say anything like that about Joie again. If you ever do, I'll never let you set foot on this property – let alone announce!

"You could call it color-blind or anything you want, I suppose," Wickliff said years later. "We really didn't think of Joie as black or anything else. He was just a very fine driver, just one of the racing community and a great guy to be around."

It may have been a coincidence, but that afternoon Ray seemed more determined than ever. He may have only made the consolation, but he finished a surprising third in the 10-car field right behind two more experienced drivers.

Joie Ray was going to make the grade.

Soon thereafter, with Bobby Grim's assistance, Ray was wheeling the Lowell Todd Special. Grim had driven the machine earlier in his career. It was only a six-cylinder flat-head Ford, but

Left: Future two-time IMCA champion Deb Snyder poses with his powerful 318-cid Offy. Snyder figured in Ray's big win at Wausau in 1949. Right: Travis "Spider" Webb was the defending AAA Midwest Sprint Car champ when he gave Ray his driver's test at the Salem Speedway in 1949. At Spider's suggestion to the officials, Ray became the first professional black driver in history, breaking the color barrier in major-league auto racing.

weekend found him back in the Todd machine, fighting the dust and rocks with everyone else.

"I remember one race at Franklin, when Joie raced Cantrell until Bill's tongue hung out," Wickliff said. "It was in the feature. Cantrell was leading, but Joie tried him high and low, all crossed up on either side of him, but he couldn't get by. It was one of the best races I'd seen in a long time. Bill won, but Joie was right behind him in second."

In 1948, when Cantrell went to the AAA and Indy, Ray took over the cockpit of Virgil Graybeal's sprinter known as "The Southern Star." "Bill Cantrell was instrumental in getting 'The Star' for me to drive," Ray said. "It was a huge step in my career."

The Southern Star was powered by a double-overhead cam Hal conversion for the Model B Ford. Sometimes called "the poor man's Offy," the Hal was a very potent creation. Since Graybeal worked for the Armour Meat Packing Company, he adorned the tail of the racer with his employer's star logo. The car carried no numeral.

On July 3 Ray broke into the win column by taking his first feature victory at Carrollton, Ky. This was followed by a fine performance the following day at Greenville, Ohio. A few weeks later Ray and Graybeal's

sprinter won a second feature at Carrollton.

"Joie was the only driver my dad ever trusted to take the racecar to a track by himself," Jim Graybeal said with admiration. "Dad always said he was one of the best drivers he ever had in his car.

"One time, Dad and Mom were coming home from a race. Joie wanted to treat them to a fine dinner, but he knew, in that day, he'd have trouble being served in most restaurants. So, he asked Dad to stop at a place owned by some black people he knew. Well, Joie had to go in and ask permission to bring in some white people. The owner said, 'Sure,' and Mom said she never had a better meal or was treated any nicer."

While Ray found less and less resentment around the nation's speedways, traveling to and from could be another matter. One night, Chick Smith and a group of racers stopped at a motel where Smith was a regular customer. But the proprietor refused to give Ray a room.

"And after all the times I've stayed here," Smith grumbled. "You mean to tell me you won't let my half-brother sleep in my room?" The owner couldn't believe Smith was serious. "Do I look like I'm kiddin'?" the pokerfaced Smith insisted. "If my half-brother doesn't stay, I ain't staying, either!" Needless to say Ray got a bed for the night.

"All through that deal, I was just about to burst out laughing," Ray recalled. "You should've seen that motel owner's face. That Chick – he was some swell guy."

Still, it was a hard and difficult road. The obstacles were many. In a sport that often builds up a competitor's confidence only to knock him down, Ray was about to experience the grim reality of racing in that era. It was never clearer to him than on the Sunday afternoon of Sept. 19, 1948, at Franklin, Ind.

In the third heat race, Ray went to the front with a stunning, rim-riding display of driving, winning the event over Glenn "Pee Wee" Northern and Zeb Davis. Davis was an experienced hand, and not long after the race Northern would set a world record for a half-mile dirt track at Owasso, Mich. Even though Ray was riding the crest of his Kentucky successes, this victory over two such veteran drivers was a surprise to many. But it was the way he drove, his spectacular style, with The Star all crossed up and pitching dirt over the outside rail, that made this event stand out from his other wins. Cantrell and Smith had been telling everyone that Ray would soon be a contender on the circuit. Smith, who had suffered engine trouble and wasn't going to race that day, was only slightly less elated than Ray. "I told you he'd do it," Smith told an acquaintance. "That

Above: Al Fleming provided an excellent car for Ray to drive in IMCA competition. Ray drove the Fleming Hal to victory at Wausau, his most outstanding win. Below: Ray warms up the Fleming Hal sprinter at Des Moines, Iowa, in 1949.

– Ray was on the track when the race was restarted. With fierce determination, he brought the Graybeal sprinter through the field, picking off car after car in one of his best drives at Franklin. At the finish, the winner was Bobby Grim, followed by Bud Dombroski and Joie Ray.

Ray hurriedly left the track for the small hospital to be at Smith's bedside. The following day, Smith died of his injuries.

"Chick was one of the best friends I ever had and his death had a great effect on me," Ray said. "I thought about quitting then, but his wife Dorothy encouraged me to continue."

By 1949, Ray not only competed in the local series, he branched out to the larger Central States Racing Association (CSRA) and the International Motor Contest Association (IMCA). The latter group ran virtually all over the nation, counting many of the huge state fairs as regular stops. The long hauls across pre-freeway America were really tough on men and equipment. The competition, featuring the sensational Frank

Joie is really gonna go places!"

In the next event on the program, veteran driver Les Adair was killed in a two-car accident. Many of the younger men looked to the 40-year-old Adair for guidance. Friendly and personable, Les never met a stranger and had a million friends; during delays in proceedings, his jokes over the PA system entertained the fans. While his death wasn't announced to the crowd, the racers all knew of his demise. It cast a cloud of gloom over the pit area. Out of respect for their fallen friend, several drivers even withdrew from the rest of the program.

Prior to the feature race, Smith was tabbed to replace Adair's longtime friend Hank Schlosser in the powerful Doc Bowles Offy. On the opening lap, Smith was going for the lead, when his car clipped the outside rail. The racer flipped twice, tearing out nearly a hundred feet of wooden fence and a large access

gate. The hurtling machine bounced high into the air, snapped off a light pole eight feet above the ground, then slammed back to earth with tremendous impact. It was a horrifying accident. Thrown from the machine, Smith was critically injured.

True to the racer's code – the show must go on

Luptow, Emory Collins, Deb Snyder, Bert Hellmueller and the emerging Grim, possessed unbelievable talent. Collins and Snyder wheeled 318-cid Offenhausers, while Hellmueller's car was powered by a 441-inch Ranger aircraft engine and sported four-wheel drive. Running against them with a 220 Hal was no picnic.

Ray and the Bill Pendelton sprinter ready for a day of racing at Dayton, Ohio, in 1950. This was Ray's first full season with the AAA.

Ray drove several different cars besides The Southern Star, including Al Fleming's Hal.

"One time I drove for a guy who was so far down on his luck, he couldn't afford to pay his drivers," Ray chuckled. "But I drove for him anyway. I just wanted to race."

Ray was paying his dues.

Although Rajo Jack, Smokey Harris and Doc White had raced with IMCA on temporary permits, as far as can be ascertained Ray was the first black driver licensed by the organization. On June 12, 1949, Al Sweeney, president of National Speedways – a division of IMCA – signed him up at the Iowa State Fair in Des Moines.

Several years later, Grim and Hellmueller, accompanied by Sweeney and his wife, went to Ray's Louisville home, where Sweeney presented Ray with a plaque commemorating his licensing as the first black driver in association history.

The racing press of that day often referred to Ray's driving style as flashy. He was certainly smooth, and

when track conditions permitted the technique, he liked to "go upstairs," run against the outside rail, pitch a rooster tail of dirt over the fence, and put on a real show for the fans.

At Wausau, Wis., Ray and the Fleming Hal were really rolling. Giving away nearly 100 cubic inches and with half the horsepower, Ray was running a close third behind the huge Offys of Luptow and Snyder.

"The track was real dusty," Ray remembered. "They were running so hard for the lead they mistook the white flag [the signal for the final lap] for the checker. [Luptow and Snyder] slowed down, and I just went by them."

When the two veterans realized their mistake, they took after the Hal. But Ray held them off for the win.

"There's no way I could have beaten them," Ray said. "Not with those big Offys they had."

As modest as Ray was about the Wausau victory, he learned to accept such wins as they came about. Next time, fate could hand you the short end of the stick.

"I felt a little funny about winning that way," Ray

said. "But Frank (Luptow) told me to enjoy every win you get. A win is a win. And there wasn't always enough racing luck to go around."

With his upbeat nature, Ray contended he only encountered racism three times around his chosen sport. But there was one glaring example of at least collateral prejudice aimed at him.

Following the exciting Wausau triumph the local newspapers – although they always covered the IMCA races at the track – ran nothing about the event. More astonishing was the reaction of a major auto racing publication whose headline read: "Luptow and Snyder Second and Third At Wausau." In the article, there was no mention of Ray winning the race.

Ray may not have noticed, but his friends and fans were more than a little angry. But a more formidable obstacle still awaited Ray – membership in the elite ranks of the AAA.

As the sanctioning body of racing's major leagues, the American Automobile Association lorded over the sport. This was hardly the benevolent association of today that comes to the assistance of its membership to change a flat tire or jump-start a dead battery. This was a dictatorial board that ruled racing with an iron hand. If one of their licensed drivers so much as attended an outlaw program, he could face a fine. If he took part in an unsanctioned event, he could be fined, suspended for up to a year, or even banned for life. And the AAA, as with many organizations of the day, had an unwritten color barrier.

As an example, in 1910, when Barney Oldfield and his manager Bill Pickens staged a series of races against black heavyweight boxing champion Jack Johnson, the AAA banned racing's first superstar for a year. As a matter-of-fact, Oldfield wasn't allowed to compete in the first two Indy 500-mile races. By the time he was back in good graces with the AAA, Barney's talents had eroded to the point that he never regained his previous stardom.

Even in the 1930s, "Chickie" Hiroshima, who was of Japanese decent, had to obtain special permission to act as Rex Mays' riding mechanic at Indy. And that was a long, drawn-out process.

Although still bound in dictatorial rules, the postwar AAA was run under the auspices of younger, fairer-minded men. A new era was about to begin.

By the autumn of 1949, Ray had joined forces with black sprint car owner Mel Leighton. (Leighton's car was the same car in which Orville Epperley lost a leg in a grinding crash earlier in the year at Winchester, Ind.) The Ray-Leighton team's first event was set for a meet at the fast and unforgiving high-banked dirt half-mile at Salem, Ind. While Ray made several test laps running in close company with former AAA Midwest Sprint Car Champion Travis "Spider" Webb and Johnny Shackleford, who had all but clinched the '49 title, AAA officials Bob Martindale and Russ Clendenen scrutinized his every move. Having received a thumbs-up from both his test drivers, Ray was issued a full AAA license. He had broken the color barrier just as Jackie Robinson had done in baseball.

"One driver objected, but Webb and Shackleford went to bat for me," Ray said. "I only made the consolation that day, but I made sure I beat the guy who protested.

"The AAA guys always treated me great," Ray insisted.

Few drivers – black or white – could say they came from the local bullrings to the AAA in less than three years.

Probably the closest thing to prejudice Ray ever encountered from a fan came at Knoxville, Tenn. Tony Bettenhausen had won the feature. But Ray, driving an inferior machine, had been impressive. There were more fans and autograph-seekers crowded around Ray than encircled the great Bettenhausen.

"This old fellow in bib overalls and no shoes came up to me," Ray recalled. "'I wanna shake your hand,' the old man said. 'Before the race I told my wife that darkie wouldn't do any good. But you proved me wrong. Congratulations!'

"Now I think that's funny," Ray chuckled, "not discriminatory."

But in many ways, as it was for most racers, joining the AAA was like starting over. Ray drove a host of different machines. Many were not the cream of the crop by any means, and seldom made the main until he wheeled them.

On July 15, 1951, when car owner Mike Caruso's driver Charlie Ethier was late getting to the Salem Speedway, Caruso tapped Ray to warm up the potent racer. Caruso's car was a lightweight, stretch-midget sprinter powered by a supercharged Offy. Ray looked great in practice and might have won the seat in the sleek machine, but Ethier arrived in time to qualify. Later in the program, Ethier crashed to his death.

When they were on their way up – before they graduated from stock block sprinters to Offy-powered racers and Indy – Ray won his share of heat races and semi-features from drivers like AAA Midwest Sprint Car champs Pat O'Connor and Joe James, '54 Indy 500 "Rookie of the Year" Larry "Crash" Crockett and '55 Indy winner Bob Sweikert.

By the early fifties, the merely curious who watched in amazement at this rarest racing phenomenon – a black driver – had long since given way to a legion of true admirers.

Below: Ray at the wheel of Mary Hulman's potent HOW Special at the Minnesota State Fair in 1953. Right: Ray beams with approval while Lee Duran checks over his vintage racer, the Gaddis Dreyer sprint car (also opposite) at the Winchester Old Timers gathering in 1991. It had been nearly four decades since Ray had driven an open-wheel racer.

Ray had some memorable races on those frightening and lethal high-banked tracks at Salem, Winchester and Fort Wayne in Indiana, and Ohio's Dayton Speedway.

One day at Winchester – the world's fastest half-mile – Ray got a chance to drive the Bob Estes V8 Mercury-powered sprinter usually driven by Joe James. James had been finishing fifth or sixth most of the season, usually surrounded by the all-conquering Offy-powered cars. Coming from back in the pack, Ray drove a fine race, finishing fifth in the main. James hadn't done any better with the car, and it proved that Ray had what it took to be a top-notch racer. A year later – now wheeling an Offy – James was the AAA Midwest Sprint Car champ.

On Aug. 30, 1953, at the Minnesota State Fair, Mary Hulman gave Ray a chance to drive her new Offy sprinter, the famous HOW Special. Since her regular driver Jerry Hoyt had a prior race commitment, this was a one-shot deal. But Ray was eager to showcase his ability in a top car. During warm-ups, he gave the racer a spectacular rim-ride. Many who were present said Ray was faster than anyone else on the track. But when the chief mechanic insisted Ray qualify in the low groove, Ray's time was a few hundredths of a second too slow and he missed the lineup.

"The low side just wasn't the way to get around fast, that day," Ray said. "But you couldn't argue with 'Stoogie' Glidden. He'd fire you in a second for not doing what he said."

During this era, Ray was also running a Henry J in AAA stock car events. Watching him rub fenders with those big Mercurys, Buicks and Chryslers with the little Kaiser product made you realize how gutsy and determined he could be.

By the mid-fifties Ray had gained the attention of Eddie Anderson, who played Rochester on the "Jack Benny Show." Anderson was a racing fan, and he'd been watching Ray's progress with interest. The two men hit it off, and Anderson contracted Andy Granatelli to build an Indy car for Ray. But the deal fell through when Anderson's finances were tapped for a personal emergency.

After 1955, when the AAA quit racing, Ray became the first black member of the newly formed United States Auto Club, where he mainly concentrated on the stock car division. He also raced in Midwest Auto Racing Club (MARC) stock cars.

In 1963, Ray chose a race at Salem for his swan song as a driver. He took the flag in a MARC stocker and called it a career.

It had to be tough watching other drivers with whom he raced go on to Indy fame and fortune, but Ray never complained. "I had such a great time racing with those guys, I wouldn't take anything for the experience."

Ray continued to attend as many races and vintage events as possible. Your author attended many memorabilia shows, where Ray often had 10 or 12 people at a time standing around him, talking racing.

"The fans are just great," he would beam. "They come up and tell me about this or that race they saw me drive. It makes you feel real good."

In the summer of 1991, Ray attended the Winchester Old-Timers gathering, where he was introduced to vintage race car owner Lee Duran. It just so happened that Duran had recently restored the Gaddis Dreyer driven by Ray in CSRA competition. Duran offered Ray a ride.

Nearly four decades had elapsed since Ray had driven an open-wheel racer. But after some warm-up laps, he cut loose with some pretty surprising circuits, which astonished those in attendance.

"Everything was fine," Duran said of Ray's excursion back in time. "Except for the fact we couldn't get the smile off his face."

After one track session, Ray kicked the car out of gear, shut the engine down and coasted to the pits. He told Duran he noticed the oil pressure dropping.

"The last time I drove this car, it lost a rod in the number three hole," Ray told Duran. "It feels a lot like it did that day."

Sure enough, when the engine was torn down it had a loose rod in the number three cylinder.

That evening ESPN interviewed Ray on a live national broadcast. Except for hardcore fans, it's doubtful most viewers realized who he was or what he'd accomplished. But for those of us who look younger with our hats on, it was a privilege to witness his considerable daring and talent.

In 1991, Willy T. Ribbs became the first black driver to make it to Indy, and Joie Ray returned to the high, wall-like turns of the Winchester Speedway. One can guess who had the most fun.

Ray could have been bitter and hateful about the way things were in his day. But he loved the sport and the people involved. He helped an entire generation of rugged individualistic racers put aside their prejudices, perhaps to never pick them up again.

In the fall of 2006, Ray attended the Jungle Park Speedway reunion. He rode around what remains of the track where he once drove, regaling those accompanying him with stories about the legendary track.

In the spring of 2007, Ray contracted pneumonia. He was admitted to the hospital and died in his sleep on April 13. It was 60 years and one week since his debut as a racing driver. He was 84.

In 1997, on the 50th anniversary of Jackie Robinson's first major league game, his number 42 was retired from the sport.

In the case of Ray, that would be impossible. His various cars carried 2, 7, 18, 34, 94 and many other numerals. And, of course, in the case of Virgil Graybeal's Hal, no number at all – just a star. Perhaps in Ray's case, that is what should be retired. Because on or off the track, Joie Ray was certainly a star. AQ

FROM *Peking* TO *Paris*

A *full century has passed since the French newspaper* **Le Matin** *organized the Peking-to-Paris event, an enduro that lived up to its hype. The dangerous event proved, according to the first finisher Prince Scipione Borghese, that "in the present year of grace it is impossible to go by motor-car alone – comfortably seated on the cushions of the same – from Pekin(g) to Paris." Void of all comfort, however, four of five cars did finish the journey. With aid from* **The Autocar,** *we reflect on that perilous adventure. We also relive the route in 2007 through the experience of a pair of modern-day adventurers.*

BY TRACY POWELL AND PETER RÜTIMANN

The editors of *Le Matin* issued a challenge:

"What needs to be proved today is that as long as a man has a car, he can do anything and go anywhere. Is there anyone who will undertake to travel this summer from [Peking to Paris] by automobile?"

Answering the call were the following: a race-engined 7-liter Itala, a Contal cycle car, a Spyker, and two De Dion Boutons. Despite the fact that the enduro would be contested during the rainy season – and over treacherous, largely uncharted territory – the cars lacked even such basic amenities as roofs and front brakes. Plus, there were no rules. First to reach Paris won a magnum of Mumm champagne, nothing more – other than fanfare and plenty of press. The only stipulation mandated that racers uphold a gentleman's agreement to help each other in case of difficulty.

Entrants' maps illustrated a nearly 10,000-mile trip across two continents, through such diverse topography as desert, mountainous steppe, tundra and swampy forest. Cars would leave Peking on the first leg on June 10.

THE PEKIN–PARIS RUN

Robert L. Jefferson, *The Autocar*, May 18, 1907

The delightfully inconsequent manner in which the proposed motor drive from Pekin* to Paris is being discussed can, perhaps, be only properly appreciated by one who knows the greater portion of the country which it is hoped will be traversed. The proposers of the scheme seem to have gone about the preliminaries with that airy indifference to detail which one usually associates with schemes that never materialize. The route to be followed is, I understand, via Mukden and Kharbin to Tchita, where the Siberian track is joined. Thence to Lake Baikal (to be crossed by ferry), and thence to Moscow via Irkutsk, Krassnoiarsk, Tomsk, Omsk, Tuimen, Ekaterinburg, Perm, Kazan, Nijni Novgorod, and Vladimir.

Let me say that I know the whole of the "road" from Moscow to Irkutsk from two journeys, one by bicycle and the other partly by troika tarantass [a large, Russian-built four-wheeled carriage mounted without springs on two parallel wooden bars]. Going eastward, all idea of a made road ends at Nijni Novgorod. Eastward from this place to the Siberian town of Ashinsk, 6,000 kilometers away, there is not only no road, but in places there is no defined track. From Nijni to Kazan, a matter of about 400 miles, the track is a mile to two miles wide, through deep sand and swamps. In summer the loose

Left: Ettore Guizzardi, Prince Borghese's mechanic, stood all day bent over the wheel as laborers pushed and pulled the Itala over rocks and through narrow ravines. Right: The Itala passing at the foot of an ancient Chinese temple near Kalgan.

* Editor's Note: At the time, Peking, China, was named Pekin.

Above left: No alternative but to take the Trans-Siberian Railway, the Itala skirts along Lake Baikal, crewed by a policeman whose red flag is extended to stop approaching trains. It did not always work. Right: A verst pole encountered on the Siberian route. Without speedometers, the only way the car crews could judge speed was by counting the verst poles against a stopwatch. Below: Near Siberia's Lake Baikal, the Itala meets with misfortune as the bridge beneath it succumbed to the car's weight.

sand is several feet in depth; in wet weather it is impassable, and even horsed vehicles cannot proceed through the several feet of mire and water which collect. For some portion of the way the track is bestrewn with boulders and fallen trees.

The only vehicular traffic between Nijni Novgorod and Kazan is by small telegas, or two-horsed light traps with broad flanged wheels, and these can only make journeys from village to village when the weather is propitious. From Kazan to Perm the track is defined, but, remember, it is a track in the virgin soil, and has been created merely by the passage of caravans from point to point. From Perm to Ekaterinburg there is no made road, and here the Ural mountains have to be crossed.

Tuimen is the next place, and eastward from here the great Steppes of Siberia face the traveler. The Tartar steppe separates Tuimen and Omsk. Between these points, beyond the Government post stations, there are no towns or villages. The way is indicated only by the telegraph wires and poles, and without these latter the track through sand, mud, and swamp would be impossible without guides. From Omsk to Tomsk there is a little stretch of about 1,000 miles of steppe, and here again the way from post station to post station is shown only by the telegraph line. The difficulties of this steppe are, in my opinion, beyond all motoring possibilities. A tarantass may be dragged by horses through three feet of clay and mud and sand, but how a motor car under its own power will be able to encompass such country is beyond my understanding. There is mountainous country between Tomsk and Irkutsk, but until Ashinsk is reached there is no semblance of an artificially constructed road.

I do not say that a semi-motor journey from Pekin to Paris is impossible. Few things are impossible when time, money, and energy form the directorate of the scheme, but what I do say is that our French friends are taking on a job they do not know much about, and it would have been just as well if they had made a few enquiries before they launched their prospectus.

En passant, it may not be without interest to Parisian automobilists to remind them that some seven years ago a Dr. Lehwess attempted a tour of the world on a Peugeot car. The car was called the Passé Partout. As I knew the country, my advice was solicited – and scouted. I was even invited to participate in the journey, but, knowing what I knew, I told Mr. D. M. Weigel, who carried the invitation, that no motor car

Left: A Russian carriage-builder (right) shows the new wheel he made for Borghese (left) in a few hours in the forest between Perm and Kazan. Right: The postcard Charles Godard sent Spijker after his magneto was repaired. Date-stamped from Tomsk, it reads: "This is the state of my Spyker after a tough crossing of the Gobi, the Walls of China, rocks, swamps, Lake Baikal." On the back it reads: "I can assure you that if I had been helped, and if I had had the petrol, Borghese would not have been the leader, although his car is 60 horsepower."

could proceed more than 10 miles east of Nijni Novgorod. The Passé Partout reached six miles east of Nijni Novgorod, and then, over its axles in sand and mud, was abandoned, and the "round-the-world" party returned by train to Paris. Some months later, the Passé Partout was dug out of its bed by gangs of men, and brought back to civilization by Mr. Charles Friswell.

Iron Wills, Able Machines
The Autocar, June 15, 1907

The competitors in the run from Pekin to Paris are evidently finding that they are in for a harder task than they had anticipated. It was at first asserted that the Chinese and Russian authorities had carried out arrangements so thoroughly for looking after the conveniences of those who are taking part in the run that they would be able to accomplish the journey without incident. The caravan routes were in good order, and supplies of everything were to be found at the different stages, so that the jour-

ney was to be as comfortable as circumstances would permit. But during the past week or two the competitors who are in Pekin have had time to sample the Chinese route, and, judging from the cablegrams received in Paris, their enthusiasm is dwindling to vanishing point.

Soon after leaving Pekin, the road becomes a mere track, which winds through a wild mountain country up to all sorts of altitudes, and sometimes disappears altogether. The cars will have to cross ravines where there are no bridges, and climb mountain passes where there are no roads. Road construction and bridge building had not been taken into account by the competitors, who are doing the best they can by loading up the vehicles with hauling tackle, bamboos, tents, and provisions. According to Prince Scipione Borghese, who has prospected a part of the route, the mountainous region between Pekin and Kalgan is unparalleled for picturesqueness, but it will probably take eight days for the caravan to traverse the 120 miles of country, where the cars will have to be pushed or hauled by coolies.

Even the geographical difficulties are not so great as those that have been placed in the way of competitors by the Chinese Government. The organizers of the run had stated that the Government had expressed the greatest sympathy for this demonstration, and would do everything in its power to make it a success, but ever since the cars have been in Pekin the Chinese authorities have been trying to induce the intrepid motorists to take the route through Manchuria, with the idea, apparently, of shifting any responsibility on to the shoulders of the Japanese authorities. The Chinese are looking with anything but sympathy upon the automobile. The start from Pekin was to have taken place on Monday last, and probably at the present moment the five cars are grappling with unprecedented difficulties. The vehicles are a 40 h.p. Itala (driven by Prince Scipione Borghese), a 15 h.p. Spyker, two 10 h.p. De Dions, and a Contal tricar.

Borghese (left) and journalist Luigi Barzini button up before leaving Berlin.

The Autocar, June 22, 1907

According to cablegrams dispatched from different parts along the route, the party of automobilists who are driving from Pekin to Paris are going through adventures that are quite unique in the history of the motor car. When an account of the journey comes to be written, it will read more like a fable than actual fact, and it will be regarded as a foolhardy undertaking or as a sublime feat, according to whether or not the vehicles succeed in returning to Paris.

After placing all sorts of obstacles in their way, the Chinese Government had to give in to diplomatic pressure, and provide passports which would ensure for the motorists a safe passage, and they have, in fact, met with quite a friendly reception, one mandarin even going to the extent of entertaining them.

The difficulties of the journey were by no means exaggerated, and they have been further aggravated by the early setting in of the rainy season. At their best, it is difficult to imagine how the roads can be worse, but, after judging of samples from photographs, nothing but admiration can be felt for the valiant band of automobilists who have to get their vehicles along routes where they sank up to the hubs in mud. The Contal tricar was soon in difficulties, and did most of the first stage by rail. The other cars shed as much impedimenta as they conveniently could, so as to reduce the load, but even this did not allow of the vehicles getting along unaided. A little army of 150 coolies accompanied the caravan to help cars out of difficulties, while the mandarins received instructions to provide others if wanted.

So far, this remarkable run across two continents has not been a test of driving cars, but a demonstration of what can be done in the way of conveying vehicles over impossible country, while undoubtedly it proves the solidity of cars that are capable of submitting to such rough handling. As a French journalist, who is accompanying the expedition, says: "We are not, properly speaking, automobilists, but marvelous acrobats."

It has taken three days to cover less than 80 miles. Henceforth, the tourists will probably be left to their own resources, for it is hardly likely that they will be accompanied any farther by their army of coolies, and the dangers and difficulties are likely to provide the party with more excitement than is at all agreeable before getting on to civilized territory.

Prince Borghese was the first to reach Paris, doing so in his Itala on Aug. 10. Cheering crowds and an eager press corps surrounded the three-man team as the Itala approached the final destination – the offices of the Peking-to-Paris sponsor, *Le Matin*.

RESOURCES AND RESOURCEFULNESS
The Autocar, Sept. 7, 1907

The promoters of the great drive from Pekin to Paris arranged a *mise en scène* for the termination of the contest that made the arrival of the two De Dion and the Spyker cars quite as triumphal as that of Prince Scipione Borghese. Yet it must be confessed that the arrival of the Itala nearly three weeks previously – despite the fact that the Prince lengthened the journey by going from Moscow to St. Petersburg – took a good deal of gilt off the achievement of the other cars. Still, the French industry could not allow itself to lie under the shadow of another Italian victory, and everything was therefore done to shower honors upon the two French cars, with the Dutch Spyker left discreetly in the background.

Borghese enters Paris in his Itala on Aug. 10, 1907. The trip took two full months.

Cormier and Collignon certainly merited the honors that have been showered upon them, for they have displayed remarkable energy and perseverance in piloting their cars through two continents, but while recognizing the splendid qualities both of the drivers and the cars, the contest must nevertheless be regarded as a case of the Itala first and the rest nowhere. It is to be remarked, too, that Prince Scipione Borghese went through the whole run absolutely with his own resources. He declares that he had no assistance from the promoters, and that the journey cost him a small fortune. The Itala Company have decided that the car which he drove is to permanently occupy a place of honor in the works. It is never to be driven again.

The strangest thing about the Pekin-Paris event is the sudden eclipse of Godard, who was driving the Spyker car. Some of the Dutch, German and French papers have been publishing articles with a wealth of detail about Godard that would appear horribly libelous to the English public, accustomed as they are to the reserve imposed upon newspapers by the libel laws, but as Godard has tacitly admitted the facts, although pleading justification, there is nothing to hinder a repetition of some of the milder charges brought forward by the Continental Press. According to these allegations Godard, who has been associated with the automobile industry in Paris as agent for many years, induced Mr. Spyker [sic] to place a car at his disposal for the Pekin to Paris run on the understanding that the whole of the expenses were to be defrayed by the promoting journal. The *Matin* of course made no such stipulation. It offered to facilitate the journey by arranging for supplies of petrol along the route, but all expenses were to be borne by the travelers themselves.

Not having a penny in his pocket Godard sold the spare tires and parts to enable him to reach Marseilles. He there succeeded in getting credit from the shipping company to carry him and his car to China, and on arriving at Pekin with absolutely nothing he is said to have borrowed money from a bank to be guaranteed by the prize he would receive on reaching Paris. As a matter of fact, there was to be no prize at all.

[De Dion drivers] Cormier and Collignon are both full of praise of the energy displayed by Godard in getting his car through China and the Gobi desert. When stranded by the failure of the magneto he succeeded in some way in transporting himself and his car by rail to Tomsk, where he was received like a prince. He was two weeks at Tomsk waiting for a Dutch mechanic to bring another magneto, and then returning to the point where he boarded the train he accomplished prodigies in the way of driving until he caught up to the De Dion cars.

On reaching Germany he was met by Mr. Spyker, who disembarked him from the car, which was placed in charge of the mechanic. Our French friends regard Godard as something of a hero. The task of piloting a car from Pekin to Paris was hard enough for those who had plenty of resources behind them, but the way in which Godard secured the loan of a car in Amsterdam, and, with absolutely nothing to start with, journeyed halfway round the world to China, and then drove in the face of incalculable difficulties to Europe, puts all other achievements in the way of globe girdling by destitute travelers in the shade.

For a roundup of the 1907 event, see *Automobile Quarterly* Vol. 4 No. 2, "The Race to Beat All."

In 2007, a 100-year commemorative run retraced the famous event. Above is current construction of a giant Genghis Khan tribute in Mongolia.

PEKING TO PARIS, 100 YEARS LATER

A race to celebrate the centennial event took place in 2007, called "The Peking To Paris Motor Challenge 2007" organized by the Endurance Rally Association. The 130-plus antique and classic cars ran along a similar route. We caught up with enthusiast Peter Rütimann and photographer Michel Zumbrunn after they completed their run.

Peter Rütimann, Aug. 10, 2007

The invitation to take part in the Borghese Memorial event, a hundred years after that great adventure, was irresistible. The prospect of driving through eight time zones, through nine countries, over a distance of more than a third of the world circumference was incentive enough to join in. My copilot, Michel Zumbrunn, was also looking forward to riding in one of the classic cars he had admired through his camera lens for 25 years. For him it would be a new experience to realize the prospect of contributing to the book project *Peking to Paris After 100 years*.

Notable among the 2007 entrants was a period Spyker, honoring the original piloted by Godard and accurately representative down to its paint scheme.

When the 30 cars were shipped in Basel, I noticed that about half the cars did not have the prescribed 25cm ground clearance, among which were an Austin Healy and a Triumph TR4. How would they fare on the offroad tracks of the Gobi desert?

We were given an impressive reception in Peking where young and old kept crowding around the old cars inspecting the motors and admiring the interiors. People in China have only really gotten used to cars in the last 15

years. Oldtimer models from 1913 to 1966 had never been seen before. We witnessed the same interest in our caravan in Mongolia.

During the first 4,000 km in northern China we had the opportunity of visiting many cultural sites, unfortunately only along the highways with enormous road signs we could not decipher. Thanks to our Chinese guide in the Toyota, we reached our destinations, comfortable four- and five-star hotels with safe parking lots. Over the radio we often heard our tour guide Itang

warning us in perfect German: "Hello you all, mind that farmer on his bicycle," or "Take care, there's a large boulder on the roadside," or "Next exit on the right and then stop!" We continued this way for two weeks always under a grey smog cover, without ever having seen the sun. We drove past unsightly industrial complexes, which had been concealed by planting four to six rows of trees along the highway.

The 1940 Buick Eight coupe we were driving did its best to master the offroad track. This was only possible by spending several nights renewing the electric cables. Driving at 60 to 70 km/h was not ideal, as the Buick needed more air stream to cool it at temperatures of around 39 C. I tried to solve this problem by placing small wooden blocks on either side of the bonnet. With my Swiss Army knife I whittled eight such blocks, but due to the countless potholes the bonnet kept popping up.

We finally reached the Mongolian frontier, the landscape gradually turning into grassland, under a blue sky and glaring sunshine. The Gobi desert begins immediately after the frontier, which we crossed far too late due to trouble at the customs checkpoint. After two hours on the offroad track, four cars gave up. The real adventure began with a night in the desert for which we were totally unprepared; to make this worse, we had not a clue where we were. We decided that our cars were not up to following the route along the Gobi desert.
This was disappointing, as a week's experience in the desert would have been

an absolute highlight. However, the general opinion of most participants was: "We all want us and our cars to arrive safely

in Paris." And so we crossed the desert following the route taken by Prince Borghese a hundred years before. Even so, we had sufficient problems including: defect oil sumps that had to be welded in the middle of the desert; a cabriolet half-buried in a sandpit (it took 20 men to pull it out); and of course countless ruined shock absorbers. To top it all, we had to camp in the middle of a sandstorm.

Mongolia is an absolutely fascinating country with the exception of its capitol Ulaan Baatr. The Gobi desert is an experience I would like to repeat, but preferably in a modern 4x4.

A further highlight was driving through east Siberia with vast Lake Baikal and the fascinating towns built in the twenties by the wives of deported opponents of the tsardom. I firmly believe in the great future of Siberia, due to the fact that around 30 percent of the world's mineral resources are to be found there. It took us

109

25 days to cross Russia where we were able to see highly interesting ancient towns like Kazan with its striking Kremlin, and Wladimir with Russia's oldest cathedral. Moscow was not to my liking; I found it to be an unfriendly, ostentatious town. On the other hand, St. Petersburg alone was worth the trip. What an attractive, fascinating city, very much oriented towards the West, full of culture packed in striking architecture. This did not leave us enough time to see as much of the Baltic States as we would have liked, but Talinn with its intact old part of the town was a real discovery.

We then drove through Poland to Warsaw where we were impressed by its modernistic architecture, the result of the fact that the town had to be completely rebuilt, having been reduced to rubble in 1945.

And then on to Germany, with a memorable reception in Berlin given by the Swiss embassy. Driving from Berlin to Sinsheim in the pouring rain was unique – not one breakdown.

Finally on Aug. 10, we were received in style at the Place Vendôme in Paris by our friends and families. How happy we were to have reached our goal in good health and without any accidents; this all the more, as we had seen the remains of terrible accidents with trucks along our way.

These two months on the road were a great social experience, seeing how the participants grew to be a compact team, ever ready to help one another when necessary. Many of the team had to get used to the fact that there were several "alpha animals" in the group. In the end, all in all, this was an adventure I shall never forget! AQ

Birth of the GM Tech Center

T hroughout most of its history the General Motors Engineering and Styling sections were like robust youngsters, growing out of their clothes too often for their parents to keep up. Mountains of work were toiled over and completed in confined spaces. Soon after WWII, however, workers would be able to avoid stumbling over each other during a day's work; more so appreciative were the designers, whose cramped studios were no more.

BY TRACY POWELL   Adapted from *General Motors Styling 1927-1958*

An interesting group of high-level professionals gathered at a luncheon at the Waldorf-Astoria on July 24, 1945. Present at the "More Jobs Through Research" luncheon was a group of scientists, educators, editors, engineers and industrialists. Attendees from GM included Alfred P. Sloan, chairman of the board; Charles F. Kettering, head of research; and Charles E. Wilson, president.

When Sloan made his speech, he announced for the first time to the public the intentions behind a major facility expansion project, the General Motors Technical Center. "This new Technical Center," Sloan declared, "represents long-considered plans of General Motors to expand at the right time and on a broad scale its peacetime research, engineering and development activities, and even more progressively pursue its postwar policy of continual product improvement."

The facility would consist of four general staff organizations: Research Laboratories, Engineering Staff, Styling, and Manufacturing Development, in order respective to seniority. A branch of Manufacturing was a fifth unit, the Technical Center Service Section, which handled maintenance of the physical plant.

"The end objective is more and better things at lower prices, thus expanding job opportunities to an advancing standard of living," Sloan continued. "Modern science is the real source of economic progress. It has brought within reach of more and more people more comforts and conveniences, more leisure and more and better job opportunities. There can be no ceiling on opportunity if science continues to move forward. It is to accelerate the progress of scientific advancement that the General Motors Technical Center is dedicated."

The idea for such a construct dedicated to research had its spark long before that meeting. In the youthful General Motors organization, Charles F. Kettering knew how well a dedicated industrial laboratory served inventive minds and, for that matter, industrial progress itself. In the early days of Dayton Engineering Laboratories Company (Delco), Kettering realized that production, service and kindred problems in the manufacture of self-starters didn't blend with advanced engineering and research. They were separate and

Above: This aerial photo of the GM Tech Center taken in the '50s shows many interesting features of the campus, including one of the most identifiable buildings, the domed Styling Auditorium at left. Below: News crews and a large audience focus on President Dwight D. Eisenhower as he gives a speech during the dedication ceremony of the Tech Center, 1956.

distinct functions.

When he began directing GM's research efforts, Kettering wanted his staff to have no product authority or responsibility, together with enough budgetary freedom to underwrite research projects. Kettering knew that advanced engineering and research would produce more than adequate dividends.

"Facilities are only a part of the story of the Technical Center conception," Kettering said at the luncheon at the Waldorf-Astoria. "The more important factor has not been overlooked: the men to use these new facilities, the men who can make ideas grow into material things. We know the problems of the future are going to require for their solution not only the best facilities but the ablest men to use them intelligently."

On Oct. 23, 1945, on a 320-acre site north of Detroit in Warren, Mich., a groundbreaking spade turned the first sod for the Technical Center's drainage system. Soon afterward came the earthmovers.

Left: Inside the Design Center's Color Studio, circa 1956, designers were surrounded by floor-to-ceiling windows for optimum light balance. Designers selected from 4,000 choices on the left. Right: Inside the Engineering Drafting Room.

From the beginning the overall plan for the new facility embraced a number of series of structures to house laboratories, offices, drafting rooms, test cells and dynamometers. If GM had an unquestioned reputation as an industrial innovator and developer, it followed that its new installation should reflect functionality and architecturally a departure from tradition. If the Technical Center was to be a facility, it was also to be a striking, unique symbol. It would not only contain the latest, most up-to-date equipment, but it would also possess a scenic beauty, an atmosphere attractive to the people assigned to work there.

To create this combination of features, GM commissioned Eero Saarinen & Associates to conceive the architecture. The firm of Smith, Hinchman & Grylls, Inc., was named architect-engineers, and Bryant & Detwiler Co. became general contractor. Thomas D. Church was named landscape architect.

For a time, construction was held up. First, postwar steel shortages proved a speed bump. Then came material shortages resulting from the escalation of Korean hostilities.

Excavations for the first buildings – for the Engineering Staff – finally began in July 1949. Staff began moving into their new quarters by late the next summer.

The last building group to be constructed was for Styling. Harley Earl, now with an official title of vice president in charge of Styling Staff, and his former assistant, Howard O'Leary, spaded the first earth for the Styling Studio and Shop Building on Feb. 23, 1953. Construction of the Styling Administration Building began July 1953 and work on the Styling Auditorium was under way in October 1954.

Styling moved into its new headquarters on Sept. 16, 1955. That date, for all practical purposes, unofficially marked the completion of the Technical Center. It was an historical high point marking the settlement of all GM general staff organizations on the Technical Center site, as provided in the original plans for the facility. All told, 26 buildings were erected, ranging from gatehouses to large labs. On its architectural merits alone, the Technical Center instantly created international buzz and was cited as a prototype of the industrial environment of the future.

The formal dedication of the Tech Center was held May 16, 1956. The event included an address by President Dwight D. Eisenhower, which was broadcast via close-circuit TV from Washington.

The architects tapped Styling for some interesting "firsts" in building construction and use. One such "first" was overhead. Buildings at the Tech Center had luminous ceilings, especially dramatic as softly gleaming areas at night, and the first developed completely luminous ceilings using special modular molded plastic pans. They were developed by Styling to answer special needs of the Tech Center, involving automotive design and extensive drafting with no reflections or shadows. These ceilings were subsequently used in other modern buildings.

One important consideration throughout the campus was color, and plenty of it. The use of multiple, yet consistent application of color was two-fold: To give unity to the jumbo project and yet allow for individualization of buildings within it and as an element to make a beautiful industrial environment instead of a drab, monotonous one. Brilliant color found on exterior glazed bricks is carried inside and throughout the interiors. Each building had its own color key.

One of the most beautiful interiors was the corridor in the Styling Studio Building. The wide corridor was white bathed in cool light. At certain intervals, recessed back from the corridor, floor-to-ceiling panels were installed to fold back so cars may enter the studios. Each of these battery of panels sports a different hue – one set of greens, another a group of reds, and so on. Eighty-three different colors add to this organized, and therefore not garish, rainbow effect.

Upon completion of the studios, Styling had comfortable quarters from which to head design for each of GM's divisions: Chevrolet, Pontiac, Oldsmobile, Buick, Cadillac, GMC Truck & Coach, as well as Frigidaire Division and other non-automotive divisions. Each of the 16 design studios, with clear glass windows, was essentially a large drafting room, about 80 ft. long by 55 ft. wide with drafting tables by the windows and free space for many full-sized clay models or actual automobiles.

Four sets of blackboards, which moved up and down, lined the side walls under acoustical panels near the ceiling. And because designers worked with shiny, finished automobiles as well as clay models, the need for a continuously glowing ceiling – which would not create unnatural reflections on the car's surface – was satisfied in a luminous ceiling with deeply recessed fluorescent tubes behind the specially molded plastic pans. They gave 95-ft. candle at desk height and there were no shadows.

In the Styling group of buildings at the south end of the Technical Center, the architects' intention was to create buildings closely tied to 20th century technology and yet achieve appropriate atmosphere for creative rather than mechanical arts. The group of buildings consists of an Administration Building, a Studio and Shop Building, a one-story connecting garage building surmounted by a roof garden and Color Studio, an auditorium and an outdoor display yard.

Visitors entering the lobby of the Administration Building are immediately introduced to the building's unique "personality," laid vivid by a main staircase as a visual climax. The spectacular staircase is an example of large-scale technological sculpture, as modern-looking today as it was in 1953. Broad, white, rectangular treads (each terrazzo slab 7 ft. 4 in. wide) are suspended from pencil-thin stainless steel rods over a travertine pool, 60 by 16.5 feet, of flowing water. The handrail is of teak.

At the time the Administration Building was completed, brightly colored furniture covered in soft, kid leather, accompanied a 50-ft.-long and 9-ft.-wide rug, rose-colored, with a section that could zip off to allow the display of an automobile at the far end of the lobby. The reception desk was a fiberglass "flying saucer" bowl-shape about 11 ft. in diameter. A stainless steel mural by Buell Mullen graced the wall behind the desk.

Executive offices often included sculptures and other art from famed design houses such as Finn Juhl and Mia Grotel, the latter of which supplied special ceramic planters. In Harley Earl's office, cherry wall paneling featured ribbed aluminum, which contrasted with a ceiling covered in beige fabric, cross-hatched with cherry strips, according to Earl's grandson Richard Earl. Mistearl's desk provided the most delight: several

The new executives' offices were spacious and well equipped. Here, Harley Earl's office before his retirement in 1958.

gadgets were installed in the desk, including light and temperature controls, TV controls, and a desk lamp that rose from its flush position at the push of a button.

Between the Administration Building and the Studio and Shop Building was built a spacious one-story garage of glazed gray brick with an entire plate-glass side. On the garage's roof were two glass-lined corridors connecting the two main buildings. Between these, in the 150-ft. by 110-ft. space, was one of the most attractive areas at the Technical Center, a verdant roof garden, now very much in vogue. This space of gently sloping grassy carpet originally featured holly and bay berry bushes and five large trees including weeping cherry, weeping crab and Japanese split-leaf maple.

The Color Studio was constructed with a steel framework glass-enclosed "faceted circle," 78 ft. in diameter. Within this circular building were two other circular forms, one closed and one open. The closed form, 14 ft. in diameter, had a wall of pressed, patterned anodized aluminum. Here, special lights gave absolutely true color in the Interior Color Matching Studio. The acoustic walls of the small room were of ribbed white plastic.

The open form was a bit of a surprise. Virtually a glass-enclosed hole in the building, open to the sky, it was designed with a 24-ft.-diameter circular, steam-heated, blue-lined pool with a sculpture designed by Styling personnel. Functional as well as beautiful, this glass-enclosed inner area was meant to allow staff to see color in daylight, even when, in the interests of secrecy, the draperies around the outer glass wall were closed.

As high-tech as it came, six large electronically rotating display panels, capable of holding and rotating 3,888 color samples, were installed on one side.

Another variation of the aforementioned luminous ceiling was created for the circular Color Studio. The ceiling was made of white plastic "egg crates" of 1-in. hexagons. The result was an even, shadowless light. No joints were visible, and it adapted well to the shape of the building. Below, three low steps around the circumference of the building led down from the broad landing to the main floor area.

In the Studio and Shop Building, under a span of 80 ft., were the spacious metal and woodworking operations. Polished-edge grain maple floors and pale beige color on the machines gave the whole area a quiet atmosphere, appropriate for highly skilled work. The shops were outfitted with underfloor ducts for removal of dust, wood chips and scraps, leaving overhead space free of any exposed ductwork. All dust and wood chips were directed to collectors in the basement, a smart arrangement.

Styling also required a dome-covered auditorium simulating sky conditions for display and study of automobiles. Correct color can only be observed by the human eye in natural light, after all. Understanding that an automobile is essentially a colored mirror that reflects its source of light, and that to best see it is on the street and under the ideal conditions – which would be on a desert with an overcast sky – it was determined that models must be studied under the sky. An indirectly lit sky dome was the answer.

The dome, 65 ft. high with a 188-ft. span, was the first steel dome for an auditorium constructed on the pressure-vessel construction system. The steel sheets were 3/8 of an inch thick – as thin in relation to their area as 1/30 of an eggshell to its area. Above the steel were insulating material and aluminum-sheathed plates. Inside this outer dome, the inner sky-dome of 1/8-in.-thick perforated steel was suspended.

The extraordinary lighting system, composed of 140 1,000-watt incandescent lamps and 140 500-watt mercury vapor lamps, could be brought from darkness up to daylight of 140 foot-candles at the entire floor level. The lighting worked on dimmers. Near the center of the dome were positioned four openings for "cannon spots" of 3,000 watts each, any of which could be reached at any point.

The further accentuate the "stage" on which models would be arranged, the auditorium floor was covered with a medium-gray vinyl. The stage, 100 ft. long by 40 ft. deep, held three turntables, each 16 ft. in diameter, and a projection screen, 11 by 14 ft., which sank down below the stage on an elevator mechanism. The back of the stage was a glass-window wall, so that the stage also acted as a viewing stand to the open display yard beyond. Leave it to Earl and his lieutenants to further dress this central area with flamboyance: the stage curtain was made up of 1/3-in.-wide stripes of gold, silver and gunmetal braid.

One entrance to the auditorium, at the west side of the facility, was large enough to admit the largest horizontal vehicle made to date.

The auditorium was used for more than demonstrating and inspecting automobile design. It was also used for movies, slide presentations, and for receptions and banquets where 800 to 1,200 people could be seated for serving as well as for automobile display and study. To accommodate the guests, kitchen facilities were situated at the west side of the facility.

At the north end of the auditorium was a conference lounge with a curved table that sat 30 people. This room overlooked a private garden.

The elevator that conveyed staff and guests to the auditorium was a room in itself, with walls of baked enamel and with gold reflectors. It also contained a turntable. A car could be loaded on it from the end of the tunnel leading to the shop area and discharged at the level of the auditorium floor, or at the raised stage level, or at the level that led to the outside viewing yard.

This 550 by 215-ft. display yard contained the auditorium within its expansive surrounding wall that reaches 9 ft. 6 in. (The auditorium also had its own entrance marquee outside the yard.) Against the interior of the gray glazed brick wall was planted a line of Chinese elms. A pedestrian walk, paved with a specially developed dark brown-red hexagonal brick, encircled the court.

At the farthest south end of the yard were complete audio-visual facilities. A coaxial cable ran underground from the auditorium to this point, enabling a television truck to plug in at this end of the court while the cameras televised in the interior. There were also three turntables in the brick area at the far south end of the court.

If ever there was a defining moment for "backyard entertainment," this was it. And if ever there was an opportunity for GM Styling to leap forward in its endeavors, thanks to the ample room and custom-made quarters, that time was nigh.

Today, Ed Welburn sits at the same desk Earl did. Same office, very updated equipment. Not all of the controls work now, but the office is still in its original form, as are much of the Styling Section buildings, now Design Center. Mark Leavy, global director of design center operations, occupies O'Leary's old office, a suite accompanying Earl's old digs. According to Leavy, the design lobby was given a massive overhaul to re-incorporate some of its architectural heritage for one of GM's recent awards ceremonies, Eyes on Design, for the campus's 50th anniversary in 2006.

"Hopefully this is making people aware of the historical significance of this campus, of where it's been and where it's going," Leavy noted in *Detroit Auto Scene*. "Every day I feel blessed to work in this department, and in the space I have, recognizing how historical that it is … it's quite a spectacular feeling." AQ

The 550 x 215-ft display courtyard came equipped with complete audio-visual capabilities at one end, as well as three turntables in the brick area at the far south end.

NOTES AND N&C COMMENTARY

CONTACTING AQ

Automobile Quarterly, ISSN 0005-1438, ISBN 1-59613-056-3 (978-1-59613-056-2), is published quarterly by Automobile Heritage Publishing and Communications, LLC. Editorial and publication offices: 800 East 8th Street, New Albany, Indiana, USA 47150. Telephone (812) 948-AUTO (2886); fax (812) 948-2816; e-mail info@autoquarterly.com; Web site www.autoquarterly.com.

SUBSCRIPTION SERVICE

For subscriptions, back issues, indexes, reader service, changes of address, and order entry, call (866) 838-2886. If calling from Indiana or outside the U.S., call (812) 948-2886. Back issue prices start at $25.95, plus shipping. For domestic subscription orders: 1 year (4 issues), $79.95; 2 years (8 issues), $149.95; 3 years (12 issues), $199.95. for Canadian orders: 1 year, $99.95; 2 years, $189.95; 3 years, $259.95. For all other international orders: 1 year, $109.95; 2 years, $209.95; 3 years, $289.95. Mastercard, Visa, or American Express are accepted. Order online at www.autoquarterly.com. To order by mail, please send check or money order to *AQ/Automobile Quarterly*, 1950 Classic Car Circle, P.O. Box 1950, New Albany, IN 47151. The fax number for orders is (812) 948-2816.

POSTMASTER

Please send all changes of address to: *Automobile Quarterly*, P.O. Box 1950, New Albany, IN 47151. Periodical postage paid at New Albany, Indiana, and at additional mailing offices.

LEGAL NOTICE

OPPORTUNITY

Details of fund raising programs for car clubs and automobile museums are available by calling: (812) 948-AUTO (2886).

Cover & Contents

Art by Larry Stephenson.

Frontispiece

For more information on what's hot in Detroit, including "The Year of the Car" celebrations, visit www.motorcities.org and www.woodwarddreamcruise.com. Photo courtesy of Gridd Images.

Alfa Romeo Portfolio

The author wishes to thank his friends Roger Gloor, Max Stoop, Oskar and Fridel Keller, Bernhard Brägger, Adriano Cimarosti, Urs Paul Ramseier, Robert and Edgar Braunschweig, Bruno Picco and many others for sharing with him over the past 40 years knowledge and information on the great marque Alfa Romeo. A special appreciation is due to Michel Zumbrunn, who supplied the outstanding photographs used in the article and offered additional information on various cars.

As mentioned in the introduction, the list of Alfa Romeo books and articles published is very long indeed. Therefore only some of the most important publications used in preparing the article are mentioned below:

Alfa Romeo – Tutte le Vetture dal 1910, Luigi Fusi, 3rd ed. 1978;

The Alfa Romeo Tradition, Griff Borgeson, 1990;

The Immortal 2.9 Alfa Romeo 8C2900 A&B, Simon Moore, 1986;

Grand Prix, Adriano Cimarosti, 1992;

Le Alfa Romeo di Merosi et di Romeo, Luigi Fusi, 1985;

Le Alfa Romeo di Vittorio Jano, Fusi, Ferrari & Borgeson, 1982;

Alfa Romeo – Disco Volante, C.F. Bianchi Anderloni, 1993;

Alfa Romeo 6C1500/1750/1900, Angela Cherrett, 1989;

Alfa Romeo 8C2300, Angela Cherrett, 1992;

Mille Miglia 1927-1957, Conte Giovanni Lurani, 1981;

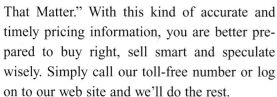

VOLUME 47 NO.4

Le Mans, A.D. Clausager, 1982;
Katalognummer der Automobil Revue – 1947-2007.

Various periodicals: *Automobile Quarterly, Automobil Revue, Fanatique de l'Automobile, Quattroruote, Ruoteclassiche, Automobil Chronik, Swiss Classics*.
Color photography by Michel Zumbrunn.

Orazio Satta Tradition

This story was excerpted from the same-titled chapter found in *The Alfa Romeo Tradition* by Griff Borgeson, published by Automobile Quarterly in 1990.

All photography from the AQ Photo and Research Archives.

Art Gallery with Larry Stephenson

Special thanks goes out to artist Larry Stephenson, whose youthful vision combined with the nostalgic is hopefully well represented here. During the interview for this story, Larry and his wife Sheryl were preparing to leave for a fishing trip in the Gulf of Mexico; Larry caught a 27-inch Red Fish (shown here) and Sheryl caught a 29-incher. "We had a blast and returned all of our fish back to the sea to fight another day."

Color photography courtesy of the artist.

Contact Information

Larry Stephenson
324 Lakecrest Drive
Andover, KS 67002
Phone: 316-733-9654
E-mail: lstephenson3@cox.net
Web site: www.lstephenson.com

Pratt Institute

The author wishes to thank Walter Holle for helping him to find his way with this story, and Marianne Brunson Frisch for introducing him to the work of Richard Arbib. Special thanks to Martin Skalski and Matt Burger for opening up their department and their patient tutelage; to Jim Quinlan, Alexandra Dymowska, John Cafaro and Molly McGee for sharing their experiences and work; Michael Albano at GM for sharing historic images; and, once again, the wonderful Mary Ann Torner for holding open the door at GM, as well as everyone who generously provided access to images.

Black-and-white photography: p. 54 courtesy of the Pratt Institute Archives; p. 63 from the AQ Photo and Research Archives.

Color photography: pp. 52, 53, 55, 56 (top left), 58, 61, 62 (bottom), 64 copyright Bob Handelman; p. 56 (top and bottom right) from the AQ Photo and Research Archives; p. 57 (top left) courtesy of Tucker Viemeister; p. 57 (top right and bottom) courtesy of Marianne Brunson Frisch; pp. 59, 60, 65 courtesy of the Pratt Institute Archives; 62 (top), 63 courtesy of GM Photo Archives.

Bibliography

Edsall, Larry, "Horbury Knows What Makes Brands Tick," *Automotive News*, October 1, 2007;

Egan, Philip S., *Design and Destiny: the Making of the Tucker Automobile*, ON THE MARK Publications, revised edition 2003;

Hannah, Gail Greet, *Elements of Design*, Princeton

Architectural Press, 2002;

Hess, Jeffrey P., "An Interview with Richard Arbib," www.hessfineart.com, March/April 2000;

Graduate Bulletin 2007-2008, Pratt Institute;

McGee, Molly, "Dergo," Transportation Design Studio, Pratt Institute, 2007;

"New York Architecture Images," www.nyc-architecture.com, 2007;

Patterson, Jerry E., *Fifth Avenue, the Best Address*, Rizzoli International Publications, 1998;

Prescott, Joel, "Commuting with a Legend," *Old Cars Weekly*, October 2003;

Pulos, Arthur, *The American Design Adventure, 1940-1975*, MIT Press, 1988

"Taxi 07," 2007, www.designtrust.org;

Temple, David W., *GM's Motorama, The Glamorous Show Cars of a Cultural Phenomenon*, Motorbooks, 2006;

Undergraduate Bulletin 2007-2008, Pratt Institute;

Wingard, Shannon, "Designer Helps Move Macs," *North County Times*, June 8, 2007.

Riley Pathfinder

The author would like to thank the following individuals for their assistance: Dave Rowlands of Iver, Bucks, England; Terry Metson; and Bill Watson. Additional research utilized the following publications:

Autocar, Motor, Autosport, Wheels;
Classic & Sports Car, October 1985;
Riley Cars 1950-1955, Brooklands Books;

BECAUSE WOOD IS JUST WOOD.

Ordinary cordless drills are meant to do ordinary things, like drill into wood. To drill steel you've got to be made of something stronger. Our new cordless drill was designed from the ground up to make steel beg for mercy. It's perfectly balanced, fast and unbelievably powerful. Visit snapon.com/drillsteel for product specifications.

Snap-on.com

NOTES & COMMENTARY (CONT.)

VOLUME 47 No.4

Riley: The Legendary RMs, John Price Williams, Crowood Press, 2005;
RM-Series Riley, James Taylor, Motor Racing Publications, 1990;
The Riley RMH-Pathfinder: An Appreciation, David Rowlands, Iver, Bucks, 2000.

All black-and-white photography and line drawings from the AQ Photo and Research Archives.

Color photography: pp. 66, 67, 74, 75, 76, 77, 78,

80, 81, 82, 83 courtesy of the author; p. 72 from the AQ Photo and Research Archives.

The Collection of John McMullen

Many thanks go out to enthusiast John McMullen for letting us have a glimpse inside his collection.

All photography by the author.

Joie Ray

The author wishes to thank the following for their valuable contribution to the story: The late Joie Ray, Billy Ray, Jim Graybeal, Bobby Grim, Bill Cantrell, Lee Duran, Bob W. Scott, Don Wickliff and Rick Whitt.

Black-and-white photography: pp. 90, 91, 92, 98 courtesy of Billy Ray; pp. 93 (top), 96 (top) courtesy of the Phil Harms Collection; p. 93 (bottom) courtesy of Bob W. Scott; pp. 94, 95 courtesy of Bud Williams;

p. 96 (bottom) courtesy of Bob Stolze.
Color photography: p. 98 courtesy of Judith Duran; p. 99 courtesy of John Mahoney.

Peking to Paris

Special thanks to Peter Rütimann and Michel Zumbrunn for offering some details about their adventure during the 2007 Peking-to-Paris Run. Research conducted for this story included digging into period accounts in *The Automobile* as well as *The Mad Motorists* by Allen Andrews and Luigi Barzini's book recounting the original event. *Peking to Paris: The Ultimate Driving Adventure* from Veloce Publishing depicts the '07 event in vivid color and detail.

Black-and-white photography from the AQ Photo and Research Archives.

Color photography by Michel Zumbrunn.

Birth of the GM Tech Center

This story was adapted from a chapter in the just-released book *General Motors Styling 1927-1958: Genesis of the World's Largest Design Studios* by Tracy Powell, available through Automobile Quarterly.

Black-and-white photography: pp. 112, 115 (right) from the AQ Photo and Research Archives; pp. 113, 114 courtesy of GM Photo Archives.

Color photography from the AQ Photo and Research Archives.

Coda

Color photography courtesy of Michel Zumbrunn.

Michel Zumbrunn in his studio.

Back Cover

Debossment of the Riley emblem from the AQ Photo and Research Archives.

The Buick: A Complete History

Buick: a name that holds that elusive, indefinable attribute to which all motorcars aspire to but so rarely possess—an understated, incontrovertible mystique.

The people of Buick have always looked upon the marque as something special. And it was—and is. In the history of the American automobile, there is no more dramatic and significant a chapter than the Buick's.

The Buick: A Complete History, 1904 to the present, is an authoritative, intimately fascinating story superbly told by two of the most respected automotive historians, each having devoted more than a decade to researching, interviewing, documenting and recording one of the great sagas of our time. Here is a book that has become the most treasured and inexhaustible reference work on this great marque. And now, to commemorate Buick's centennial, the new sixth edition expands to include information through model year 2004.

Eight sections of Appendices include chapters on Buick racing cars; the Buick in Hollywood; the custom-bodied Buick; the Royal Buicks; heraldry and mascots of the marque; and Buick around the world, with new information on ventures into China.

There can be no finer Buick book for the office, the showroom, or home library. For the Buick builder, the enthusiast, the collector, the dealer, the owner, it will be the bible on Buick. More than 130 full-color portraits of Buicks from 1905 to 2004, with every model, every event, and every period fully covered, promises much for the Buick lover.

Ferrari: Stories From Those Who Lived the Legend

By John Lamm

288 pages
ISBN: 978-0-7603-2833-0
Price: $60.00 US
288 pages, 350 illustrations (300 color)
Available from Motorbooks
www.motorbooks.com

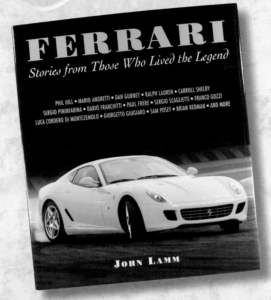

Browse through an average automotive literature collection and the Ferrari section is bound to be the most abundant. So when a new book on Ferrari was released in October 2007, the news was met with a shrug. But upon inspecting *Ferrari: Stories From Those Who Lived the Legend* by John Lamm, the unique approach to the topic is instantly seen – and appreciated.

A slew of high-profile personalities have sat in Ferrari cockpits ever since Enzo Ferrari began producing race and street versions of his cars. The unique approach comes by way of capturing a number of remembrances from these people famously associated with the marque. Legendary Ferrari figures highlighted in this book – and whose names act as individual chapters – include Carroll Shelby, Mario Andretti, Dan Gurney, Ralph Lauren and Sergio Pininfarina.

Award-winning author John Lamm is a familiar name among readers of *Road & Track* and his other nine books. In this, his latest statement on Ferrari, it is clear that much time and effort went into the compilation of interviews that comprise the meat of the book. Lamm does each individual justice by allowing the personalities to speak for their own experiences, whether on the track or at the drawing board. If one is keen to stretch the imagination, reading each person's account can be likened to sitting across a table and listening to the story, enthusiast to enthusiast.

Full-color photography throughout adds to this essential oral history. In so doing, readers are presented with a unique, multi-angled behind-the-scenes look at how the story of Ferrari took shape.

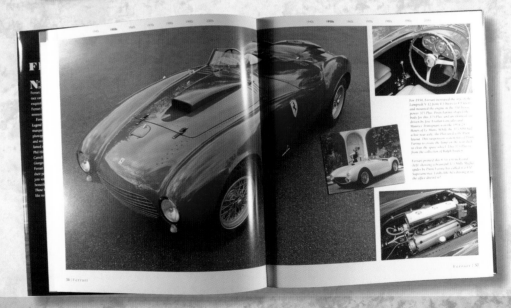

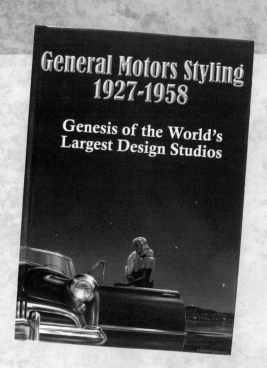

General Motors Styling 1927-1958: Genesis of the World's Largest Design Studios

By Tracy Powell

172 pages $29.95 hardcover (7 x 10)
Approx. 80 photographs (32 full-color illustrations)
ISBN 0-9709195-1-4 (978-0-9709195-1-9) 2007
Available through AQ: 866-838-AUTO (2886)
www.autoquarterly.com

A new book about the origins of GM Styling introduces readers to a world unknown to most. *General Motors Styling 1927-1958: Genesis of the World's Largest Design Studios* walks through the "Harley Earl

Above: Henry Lauve came to GM with a background in fine arts and advertising. Here we see one of the samples from the portfolio he showed Bill Mitchell. Lauve got the job and went on to accomplish much under Earl. Below: illustration of a postwar Buick idea, complete with fictious mountain brigade soldiers.

Above: Racy in more ways than one, Henry Lauve's idea of a Buick sports car. Below: A postwar consideration, conjured from Lauve's mind as World War Two raged on, a "Victory Special."

era" of automotive styling, with research and interviews that extend beyond Oldsmobile, Pontiac, Chevrolet, Buick and Cadillac, and into the extravagant dream cars and Motoramas of the '50s. Personalities leap off the page, including those who would later leave GM to make names for themselves elsewhere: Frank Hershey, Virgil Exner, Gordon Buehrig and others. They, like those who continued designing under Earl's leadership, exhibited high artistic ability combined with an eye for what would sell. They were heady days indeed, and author Tracy Powell captures the era with an apt and witty pen.

Behind the studios' closed doors, readers learn about the politics and inner workings of Earl's Art & Colour Section – later to become GM Styling – and how the

incredibly diverse melting pot of talent orchestrated standard-setting product cycles. The group of men and women would become the model for automotive design from that day forward.

More than 20 full-color artist renderings are revealed, some for the first time to the public, from the drafting tables of stylists including Bill Mitchell, Henry Lauve and Art Ross. An equal amount of telling historical photography complements the story, as does color photography of a number of milestone cars. An in-depth chapter on the birth of the Tech Center, which celebrated its 50th anniversary in 2006, covers its conception and construction. A foreword by Chuck Jordan and an epilogue by Bill Porter provide bookends for the story in between.

The story of Harley Earl has been told before. So has the history of General Motors and most of its cars. But this book takes us inside the studios, where we meet the stylists – even some engineers and executives – as if we're stepping back in time and in the thick of it.

Author Tracy Powell is managing editor at the venerable *Automobile Quarterly* and has won several awards for his writing and editing.

LIFE FOLLOWS ART

The eternal question "Does art imitate life or does life imitate art?" was partially answered in 1998 when automotive photographer Michel Zumbrunn created a photographic interpretation of Edouard Manet's famous 1863 painting "Dejeuner sur l'herbe" (Luncheon on the Grass), which now hangs in the Orsay Museum in Paris. While Manet used as models his brother Eugend, Dutch sculptor Ferdinand Leenhoff and a favorite model, Victorine Meurent, Zumbrunn did a self-portrait with two friends – and a beautiful 1949 Delahaye 135M Saoutchik in the background.

Zumbrunn entered his "recreation" in a contest sponsored by the Hasselblad Camera Company with the guidelines of producing a photograph based on a famous painting or artwork. Zumbrunn's photography won 2nd place in the contest. Today his automotive images still continue to inspire our AQ readers with their beauty and the captured spirit of the magnificent machines that pass before his lens. AQ